The Etruscans and the First Romans: The History and Legacy of the Civilizations that Fought for Control of Italy

By Charles River Editors

Luigi Garini's picture of an ancient Etruscan tomb

Introduction

A silver panel depicting Etruscan warriors

"These people of Greek descent were called Etruscans, and it has been discovered that they had advanced so far in civilization, that they afterwards gave many of their customs to the city of Rome when it came to power. A confederacy known as the 'Twelve Cities of Etruria' became famous afterwards, though no one knows exactly which the twelve were." – Arthur Gilman, *The Story of Rome from the Earliest Times to the End of the Republic*

When people think of ancient Italy, the Romans are usually the first and last people that come to mind, but long before Rome was built by Latin speaking people, the culture of Italy was dominated by the Etruscans. Although the Etruscans may not comprise the core of most histories of the ancient Mediterranean, they exerted a profound influence on the region from the 8th-5th centuries BCE that continued to resonate for centuries after as the Romans carried on many of their traditions. Today, much of what is known about the Etruscans comes from the ancient Roman and Greek writers who had a deep respect for them but saw them as exotic and foreign. As the famous Roman philosopher Seneca wrote about the Etruscans, "Whereas we believe lightning to be released as a result of the collision of clouds, they believe that the clouds collide so as to release lightning: for as they attribute all to deity, they are led to believe not that things have a meaning insofar as they occur, but rather that they occur because they must have a meaning."

The Etruscans referred to themselves as "Rasenna" in their own language, but the Greeks called them "Tyrrhenians" and the Romans referred to them as "Etrusci", which is where the modern term "Etruscan" is derived (Cornell 1995, 45). As this suggests, reconstructing Etruscan history is based primarily on the Greco-Roman accounts, but other sources are utilized by modern scholars to create a more accurate picture.

Unfortunately, despite the fact the Etruscans were a literate people, their own histories have disappeared without a trace. Nevertheless, even with this lack of primary sources, the abundance of classical writings about the Etruscans and modern historical, archaeological, and art historical studies can establish an image of Etruscan history and culture that, although not complete, is enough for scholars to arrive at some important conclusions. An in-depth examination of Etruscan history and culture reveals that the Etruscans developed a culture that was as advanced as that of their Greek contemporaries and was also one that the later Romans were indebted to on many levels.

"Rome was a poem pressed into service as a city." In that short line, Anatole Broyard, a 20th century American writer, compactly captures the timeless and enchanting beauty that resides within the Eternal City of Rome. This tourist destination is often one of the highest ranked on bucket lists, for how could one not want to experience its marvelous ruins, mirror-like rivers, and spectacular stretches of aqueducts firsthand? As one sips on fine Italian wine on a terrace overlooking the grand remnants of the Colosseum, one can practically hear the roars of the battling gladiators and the raucous applause of the spectators. And as one strolls through the coarse, yet quaint cobblestone streets, one can almost hear the galloping horses and screeching wheels of chariots in the distance, and even feel the brush of the breeze as they charge past. It is difficult not to fall in love with a city so effortlessly nostalgic it verges on utopian.

The ambitious and fearless emperors that built the legendary Roman Empire from scratch, the broad-shouldered and bronzed gladiators with their iconic plume helmets and glinting swords, and elaborate parties attended by toga-wearing Romans fueled by alcohol, violence, orgies, and other godless acts all paint a picture of Roman life. Indeed, many people are well-versed with these unique scenes of Roman history, but few are familiar with the equally riveting years preceding the dawn of the Roman Republic, and even less people are acquainted with the fabled Seven Hills sitting east of the Tiber River – the core geographical components of Rome, and the very foundations that the Eternal City was built on.

The study of Roman history is usually divided into three distinct phases: the time of the Kings, the Roman Republic, and the Roman Empire. Roman tradition dated the foundation of Rome to 753 BCE, and this first period of its history ended with the overthrow of King Tarquinius

Superbus in 510 BCE. There is very little remaining historical evidence pertaining to this period, so much of what is known is at best legend, possibly based on varying degrees of historical fact. Archaeology has uncovered some details that do tie in with the myths and stories from the era, but by and large it is a period about which little is definitively known.

The period of the Roman Republic, generally dated from 509-27 BCE, is an entirely different matter. There is significant documentation that enables historians to analyze how Rome cemented its position within the Italian peninsula before pushing ever outward to create the new provinces that formed the core of the vast Roman Empire in the third phase that came to dominate all of Europe for so long. The period of the Republic saw those with the emerging powers having to grapple with new political situations, the administration of a diverse domain while contending with political disorder at home, commercial and financial expansion, and complex issues of land distribution, the role of the military, new ideas in religion, and the emergence of new class systems. These years were certainly vibrant and laid the foundations of such characteristics as Roman discipline and the ability to adapt, as well as witnessing the formation of its political structure. The unique farmer-soldier society evolved to the extent that a few Roman citizens were able to dominate their world and time. It was not a tranquil era, but it was one in which those interested in new ideas and philosophies could thrive, and in which the conflicts between the aspirations of the great Roman philosophers and the pragmatically minded senior political and military figures drove the formation of the Roman state and provided the bedrock for its success.

The Etruscans and the First Romans: The History and Legacy of the Civilizations that Fought for Control of Italy looks at the influential civilization that helped give rise to the Romans, the origins of the Eternal City, and the war between the Etruscans and Romans. Along with pictures of important people, places, and events, you will learn about the Etruscans and early Romans like never before.

The Etruscans and the First Romans: The History and Legacy of the Civilizations that Fought for Control of Italy

The Geographic and Ethnic Origins of the Etruscans

"Adjoining these the (Alpine) Noricans are the Raeti and Vindelici. All are divided into a number of states. The Raeti are believed to be people of Tuscan race driven out by the Gauls, their leader was named Raetus." – Pliny the Elder

Determining the cultural and geographic background of the Etruscans has been a problematic endeavor for modern scholars, primarily because the cultural-linguistic grouping of their language remains a mystery. Most of the languages spoken in ancient Italy were from the Indo-European linguistic family, including Celtic, Greek, and a variety of Italic languages (among which was Latin, the language of Rome), but even though these comprised the majority of languages on the peninsula, some non-Indo-European languages were common in the western portion of Italy as well. Etruscan was one of these languages, and some scholars believe that since the language was neither "remote nor backward," it must have come from the outside (Cornell 1995, 44).

In fact, a linguistic examination of the Etruscan language can help reveal the origins of the Etruscan people. Unlike the Linear A/Minoan language, Etruscan has been deciphered for the most part by modern scholars, which is not to say that the fundamental comprehension of the language is on firm ground, but fortunately, Etruscan was still spoken and written centuries after the Romans replaced them as the dominant people in Italy, so a vocabulary of about 200 words has been compiled based on Latin-Etruscan bilingual inscriptions (Cornell 1995, 46). Another aspect of the Etruscan written language that has aided modern scholars is the fact that its alphabet was derived from the Greek alphabet, much the same as Latin (Grant 1980, 66). As such, the phonetic values of the alphabet were easier to determine for modern historians who were left to learn or (perhaps more accurately) guess the sounds of a new alphabet. Despite this, serious attempts to study the Etruscan language were largely ignored until Helmut Rix published the first basic collection of inscriptions, titled *Etruskische Texte*, in 1991 (Nagy, Bonfante, Whitehead 2008, 414). Although knowledge of the Etruscan language has helped scholars better understand Etruscan culture, as stated earlier, there are no known extant Etruscan historical texts, which means it's unclear how the Etruscans themselves viewed their own origins.

The Etruscan language has still not been linked to any known linguistic group, which has provided a dead end for academics, but archaeology may provide some answers to the Etruscans' origins. Archaeology can be used to fill in certain gaps, but it is never the complete answer to complex historical questions, such as the origins of specific cultural groups. With that said, an archaeological examination of early Iron Age Italy (ca. 1000-700 BCE) reveals that a cultural group known as the "Villanovan" was dominant. The people of the Villanovan culture were not literate, but they produced fine weapons, pottery, and most notably "hut urns" (Hencken 1968, 32-52). The hut urns resemble houses, or huts, that held the ashes of the deceased, which not only demonstrates advanced burial customs but also a fairly articulate view of the afterlife

(Hencken 1968, 28-37). The Villanovan view of the afterlife was carried on and refined even more in the Etruscan period with their elaborate tombs, as will be discussed below.

Marcus Cyron's picture of Villanovan pottery

Another picture of Villanovan pottery

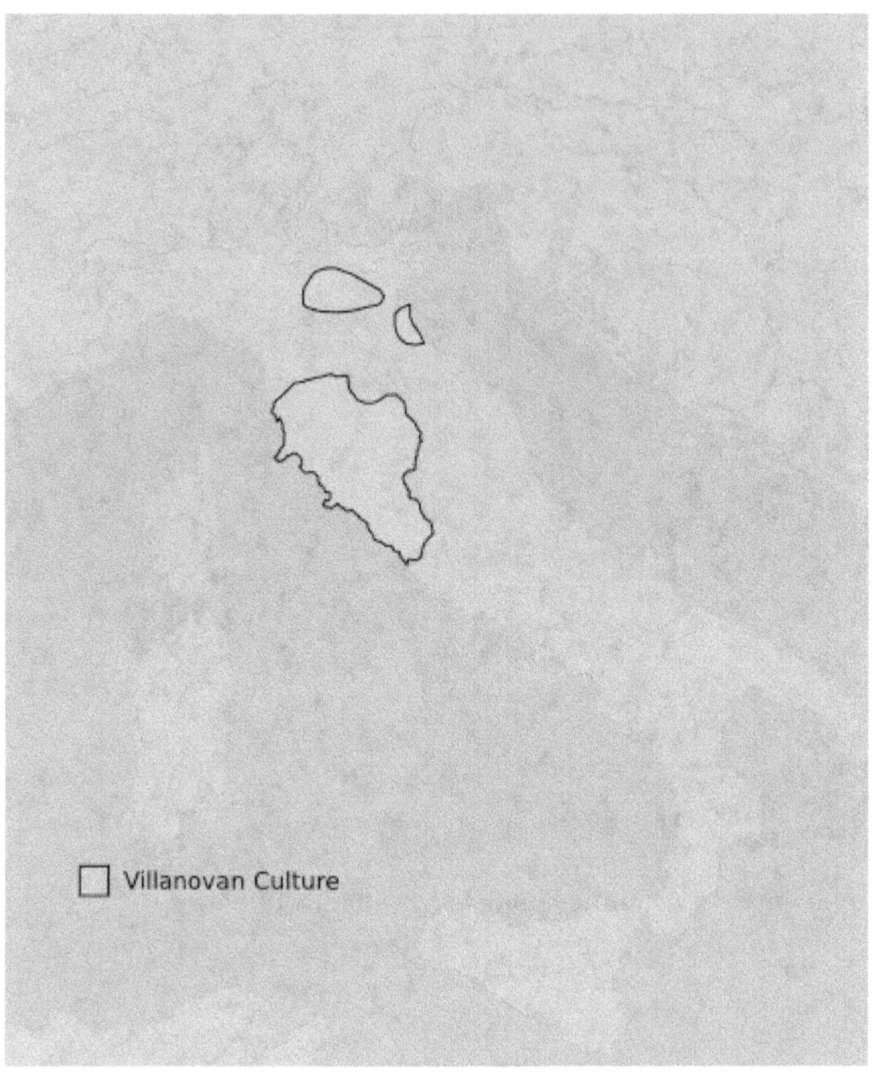

A map highlighting the area of the Villanovan culture

The Villanovan culture represented a definitive break from the preceding Bronze Age and a point where some believe the origins of the Etruscans can be traced. Currently, archaeologists agree that the transition from the Bronze to the Iron Age in the late second millennium and early first millennium BCE was definitely a technological leap, but whether or not there was a corresponding cultural shift is still debated (Cornell 1995, 31). Those who believe a major cultural shift took place point to the emergence of local cultures that permeated Italy around 900 BCE, one of which was the Villanovan culture (Cornell 1995, 33). Since most of the remains of the Villanovan culture were discovered in the region of west-central Italy known as Etruria – the Etruscan homeland – many historians believe that the Etruscans were the direct ancestors of the Villanovans (Cornell 1995, 46).

Although archaeological evidence appears to indicate that the Etruscans were descended from the Villanovan culture, it remains a question as to where, or who, they were before that. The ancient Greek and Roman writers wrote three different versions about the Etruscans' geographic origins. The Greek writers Herodotus and Dionysius of Halicarnassus both believed that the Etruscans were invaders/outsiders from different geographic origins, while the Roman historian Livy wrote that they were essentially native to Italy. Today, DNA evidence can be utilized in order to help determine what theory is the most valid.

Herodotus' account is the oldest, as he wrote his history in the 5th century BCE, and he asserted that the Etruscans were descended from the Lydian people of Anatolia. "This is their story: [...] their king divided the people into two groups, and made them draw lots, so that the one group should remain and the other leave the country; he himself was to be the head of those who drew the lot to remain there, and his son, whose name was Tyrrhenus, of those who departed. [...] they came to the Ombrici, where they founded cities and have lived ever since. They no longer called themselves Lydians, but Tyrrhenians, after the name of the king's son who had led them there…The Lydians were the first people we know of to use a gold and silver coinage and to introduce retail trade, and they also claim to have invented the games which are now commonly played by themselves and by the Greeks. These games are supposed to have been invented at the time when they sent a colony to settle in Tyrrhenia, and the story is that in the reign of Atys, the son of Manes, the whole of Lydia suffered from a severe famine. For a time the people lingered on as patiently as they could, but later, when there was no improvement, they began to look for something to alleviate their misery." (Herodotus, *The Histories*, I, 94). Although Herodotus gave no dates for the Lydian migration to Tyrrhenia/Etruria, it may have been towards the end of the Bronze Age, an era that coincided with the mysterious Sea Peoples migrations and invasions across the Mediterranean and Near East. It is even possible that Herodotus confused the Lydians with the Sea People Lukka tribe, who were also from Anatolia, but this is uncertain (Cline and O'Connor 2003, 111-112).

The 1st century BCE Greek historian Dionysius of Halicarnassus also believed the Etruscans migrated to Italy from elsewhere but attributed a different origin to them. Dionysius wrote his history centuries after Herodotus, which does not necessarily mitigate its authority, but it certainly gives the image of a different perspective. Although Dionysius was Greek, he lived under the early Roman Empire, and his audience was primarily Roman (Marincola 2004, 30). Despite the Roman influence, Dionysius was influenced by previous Greek historians such as Herodotus and Thucydides (Marincola 2004, 16), so one would expect to find similarities in his Etruscan account with that of Herodotus.

At first glance, the two accounts appear fairly different. Dionysius wrote of the Etruscan origins, "Hellanicus of Lesbos says that the Tyrrhenians, who were previously called Pelasgians, received their present name after they had settled in Italy. These are his words in the *Phoronis*: 'Phrastor was the son of Pelasgus, their king, and Menippe, the daughter of Peneus; his son was Amynotr, Amyntor's son was Teutamides, and the latter's son was Nanas. In his reign the Pelasgians were driven out of their country by the Greeks, and after leaving their ships on the river Spines in the Ionian Gulf, they took Croton, and inland city; and proceeding from there, they colonized the country now called Tyrrhenia' … For this reason, therefore, I am persuaded that the Pelasgians are a different people from the Tyrrhenians. And I do not believe, either, that the Tyrrhenians were a colony of the Lydians; for they do not use the same language as the latter, nor can it be alleged that, though they no longer speak a similar tongue, they still retain some other indications of their mother country. For they neither worship the same gods as the Lydians nor make use of similar laws or institutions, but in these very respects they differ more from the Lydians than from the Pelasgians." (Dionysius, *The Roman Antiquities*, I, 28, 3).

Dionysius' account is clearly more detailed, as he cited his sources and provided a different name to the Etruscans, but the important nuances are the same, notably that the Etruscans were forced to flee their original homeland due to disaster. In Herodotus' account, the disaster was brought on by famine, while Dionysius contends that it was the result of the Greeks.

Since neither account gives a date and archaeologists contend that the Villanovans were the forerunners to the Etruscans, it may be that both accounts were correct to a certain extent. The end of the Bronze Age ushered in a dark age in the Mediterranean region where records and knowledge were lost. At least one major famine from the period is known from ancient Egyptian historical records (Macqueen 2003, 50-51), and the Greek speaking Mycenaeans are believed by modern scholars to at least partially comprise the Sea People tribe known as the Ekwesh (Cline and O'Connor 2003, 114). With all of this in mind, it seems that both Greek historical accounts may have jumbled and conflated the confusing events of the late Bronze Age.

Of course, not all classical historians agreed that the Etruscans came from foreign soil. The Roman historian Livy, a 1st century BCE Roman historian who wrote his history in Latin (unlike Herodotus and Dionysius, who compiled their works in Greek), offered an account that directly opposed Herodotus and Dionysius. The Etruscans play a central role in Livy's books that concern the early history of Rome, but the author dedicated little room to their origins, in part because he believed the Etruscans were already in Italy at the time of the Trojan War, which modern scholars place around 1220 BCE during the migrations of the Sea Peoples (Drews 1993, 42). Livy wrote, "Trojans and Latins were rapidly becoming one people, and this gave Aeneas confidence to make an active move against the Etruscans, in spite of their great strength. Etruria, indeed, had at this time both by sea and land filled the whole length of Italy from the Alps to the Sicilian strait with the noise of her name; none the less Aeneas refused to act on the defensive and marched out to meet the enemy." (Livy, *The Early History of Rome*, 1.3).

Livy's account is augmented or possibly influenced by the Roman literary account of the Trojan War as written in Virgil's *Aeneid*. In the *Aeneid*, the Etruscans are described as essentially native to Italy and a warlike people who become allies with the Trojans. In the final battle, the Etruscan hero Tarchon is described as favored by the gods: "But meanwhile the Father of Mean and Gods, enthroned high on Olympus, had eyes to observe such a deed. The Sire stirred the Etruscan Tarchon to furious battling, goaded him fiercely on, and inspired him with rage. Accordingly, Tarchon charged on horse-back amid the carnage where the ranks were in retreat. Using every resource of appeal he urged the regiments of his cavalry forward, calling on each man by name, and rallying the routed to face the battle once more: 'Etruscans, spineless as always, are you for ever incapable even of shame? . . Having thus spoken frankly, Tarchon at the risk of his life spurred his horse into the thick of the fight, and recklessly charge straight at Venulus; he dragged him down off his horse, clasped him under his right arm, and with a violent effort carried off his enemy, holding him in front of his chest." (Virgil, *The Aeneid*, XI, 728-758).

There can be no doubt that Livy and Virgil's accounts of the Etruscans were intended, at least partially, to legitimize the origins of Rome as native to Italy, at least through its Etruscan background. For the most part, even though Rome fought a number of wars with the Etruscans, the Romans admired Etruscan culture and its influences on Roman culture.

Essentially, there is no consensus among the three major classical accounts concerning the origins of the Etruscans, but modern science may help answer the question. In 2007, Alberto Piazza, a researcher from the University of Turin, conducted a study of the DNA profiles of a number of inhabitants in the Tuscany region (ancient Etruria) of Italy. Piazza's findings show that the DNA profiles of individuals from two sub-regions of Tuscany, Murlo and Volterra, were closer to those of Near Eastern origins than other Italians (Lorenzi 2010, 36-37). In particular, one specific genetic variant is only shared with people from Turkey (Lorenzi 2010, 37). Although not all modern Etruscan scholars accept Piazza's claim of a Near Eastern origin for the ancient Etruscans (Lorenzi 2010, 38), the evidence is compelling and may serve to corroborate either Herodotus' or Dionysius' accounts. The DNA similarity of modern inhabitants of Tuscany/Etruria to those of the Near East, particularly Turkey, demonstrates that not only were the Etruscans migrants to Italy as both Herodotus and Dionysius asserted, but that they probably came from Anatolia as Herodotus stated. Of course there will always be skeptics who claim that the DNA study did not cover a large enough sample size, but when considered with the classical accounts and archaeological evidence the true picture of the Etruscan origins becomes a little clearer. Although a consensus may never be reached concerning the origins of the Etruscans, there is agreement concerning the size and composition of the Etruscans' ancient homeland in Italy.

Ancient Etruria's Topography

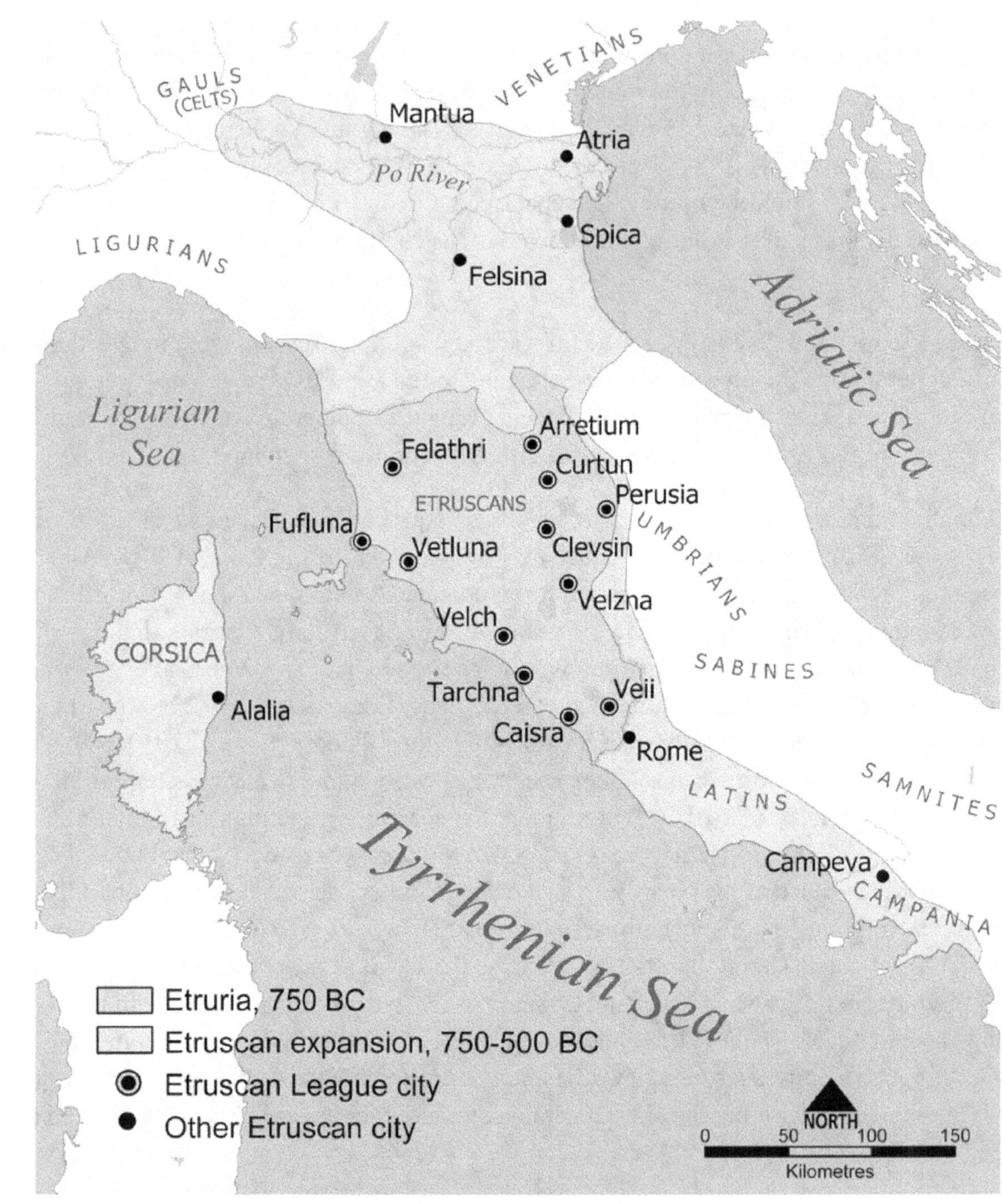

Norman Einstein's map of the Etruscan territory

A walled Etruscan town

The composition of ancient Etruria (Tyrrhenia to the Greeks) gave the Etruscans an early advantage over their neighbors because the region was so rich in natural resources. Even today, Tuscany, as it is now known, is renowned for its vineyards and agricultural output, and in ancient times, numerous historians and geographers were amazed by the abundance of Etruria and the wealth that it brought the Etruscans.

In particular, the 1st century BCE historian Diodorus wrote extensively about the material wealth of Etruria. The Greek historian noted, "The land the Tyrrhenians inhabit bears every crop, and from the intensive cultivation of it they enjoy no lack of fruits, not only sufficient for their sustenance but contributing to abundant enjoyment and luxury. For example, twice each day they spread costly tables and upon them everything that is appropriate to excessive luxury, providing gay coloured couches and having ready at hand a multitude of silver drinking cups of every description and servants-in-waiting in no small number; and these attendants are some of them of exceeding comeliness and others are arrayed in clothing more costly than befits the station of a slave." (Diodorus Siculus, *The Library of History,* V, 40, 3-4)

The fertile croplands and orchards of Etruria were augmented by an abundance of lakes and wetlands. According to the legendary ancient Greek geographer Strabo, the wetlands were a source of food and trade. "The lakes too, contribute to the prosperity of Tyrrhenia, being both large and numerous; for they are navigable, and also give food to quantities of fish and to the various marshbirds; quantities of cat-tail, too, and papyrus, and downy plumes of the reed, are transported by rivers into Rome." (Strabo, *Geography*, V, 2, 9).

Etruria was and still is, to a certain extent, a land of milk and honey; but in the ancient world people needed more than just ample food for consumption and trade in order to survive. The Etruscans clearly lived in a hostile neighborhood, as they were bordered by the warlike Celts to the north and the equally menacing Italic speaking peoples to their east (Cornell 1995, 42). Thus, in order for the Etruscans to defend their resource rich homeland, they had to develop armies and more importantly weapons for their armies to use.

Luckily for the Etruscans, their homeland was also rich in natural metals and ores (Grant 1980, 10). Most of the metals mined by the Etruscans came from the lower ranges near the Tyrrhenian Sea coastline (the Mediterranean coastline along west-central Italy), which meant that they were much easier to mine than if they were in higher, rugged mountain ranges (Grant 1980, 12). Tin was abundant, which was needed to alloy copper to make bronze (Grant 1980, 11), as well as one of the most coveted metals of the period: iron (Grant 1980, 14-17).

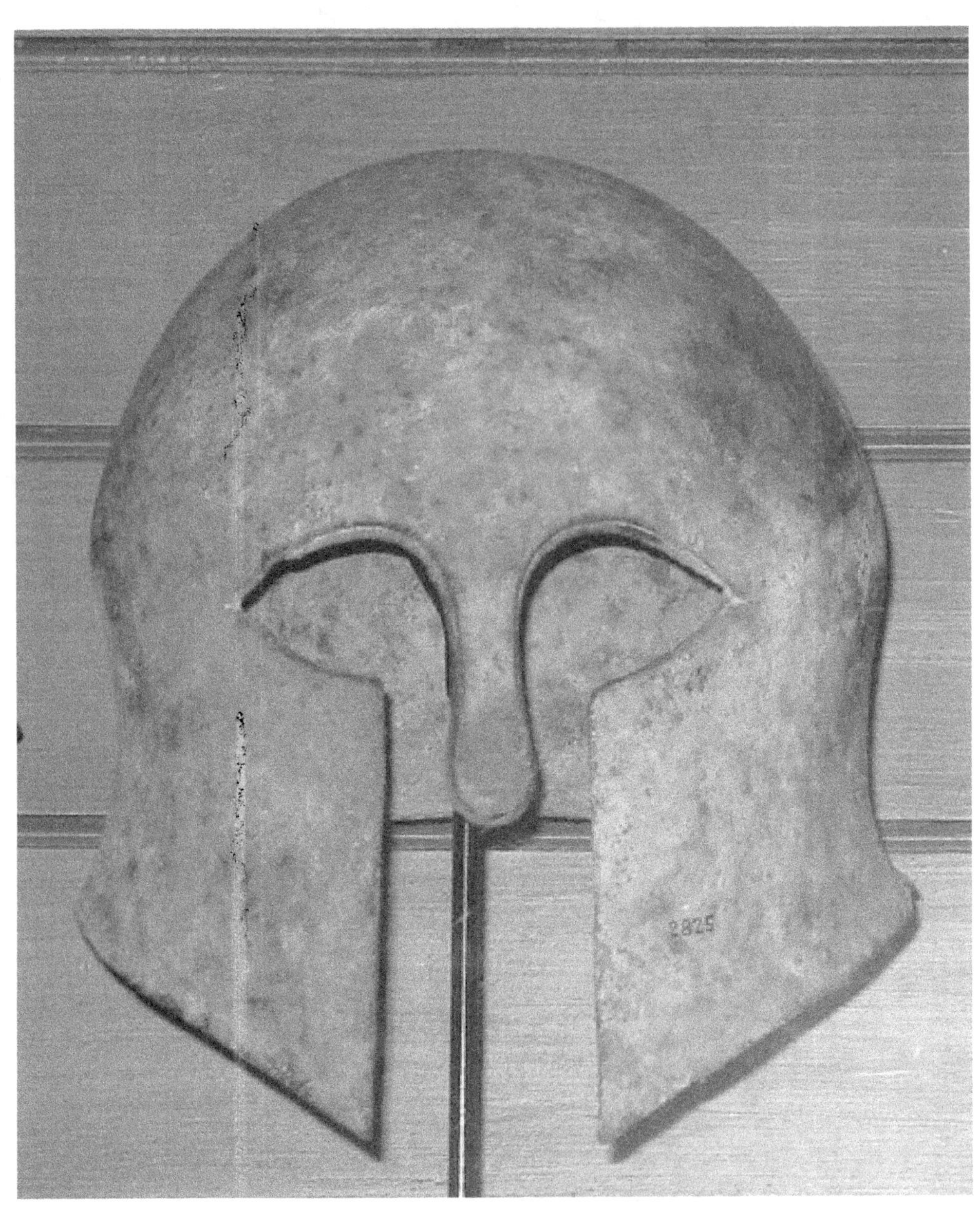

Pictures of Etruscan helmets

A 6th century BCE statue depicting an Etruscan warrior

Indeed, the presence of iron deposits in Etruria allowed the Etruscans to keep pace with their neighbors' militaries and also allowed them to expand beyond Etruria by opening new trade routes and colonies. In the 8th century BCE, the Etruscans used their metal supplies to develop trade routes with Greek colonies in coastal southern Italy, mainland Greece, and the Phoenicians (Grant 1980, 38-39). The Greek Italian market cities of Cumae and Pithecusae were founded in the 8th century around the same time that many of the Etruscan villages were coalescing into cities (Grant 1980, 40). Archaeological evidence that the foundation of Greek colonies and the establishment of Etruscan cities were connected exists in the form of pottery, but it was towards the end of that century when trading connections between the Greeks and Etruscans became solidified (Grant 1980, 46). The Phoenicians, as coastal dwelling people themselves, desired the metals more than the Greeks, so a more extensive relationship developed between them and Etruscans, which eventually influenced Etruscan artistic traditions (Grant 1980, 39).

It was also in the context of developing trade routes in the 8th century that the Etruscans began to colonize lands outside of Etruria. Etruscan colonization was not as far-flung or long lasting as Greek or Phoenician colonization during the same period, but it was observed by some of the classical writers and is worthy of mention. The Etruscans were able to expand their trade routes and colonies through a capable navy, which Diodorus noted was formidable. The historian wrote, "It remains for us not to speak of the Tyrhenians. This people, excelling as they did in manly vigour, in ancient times possessed great territory and founded many notable cities. Likewise, because they also availed themselves of powerful naval forces and were masters of the sea over a long period, they caused the sea along Italy to be named Tyrrhenian after them." (Diodorus, *The Library of History*, V, 40, 1).

Diodorus further explained that the Etruscans sometimes used their navy forcefully in their colonization efforts: "There are also on it two notable cities, the one being known as Calaris and the other as Nicaea. Calaris was founded by Phocaeans, who made their home there for a time and were then driven out of the island by Tyrrhenians; but Nicae was founded by Tyrrhenians at the time they were masters of the sea and were taking possession of the island lying off Tyrrhenia." (Diodorus Siculus, *The Library of History*, V, 13, 3-4).

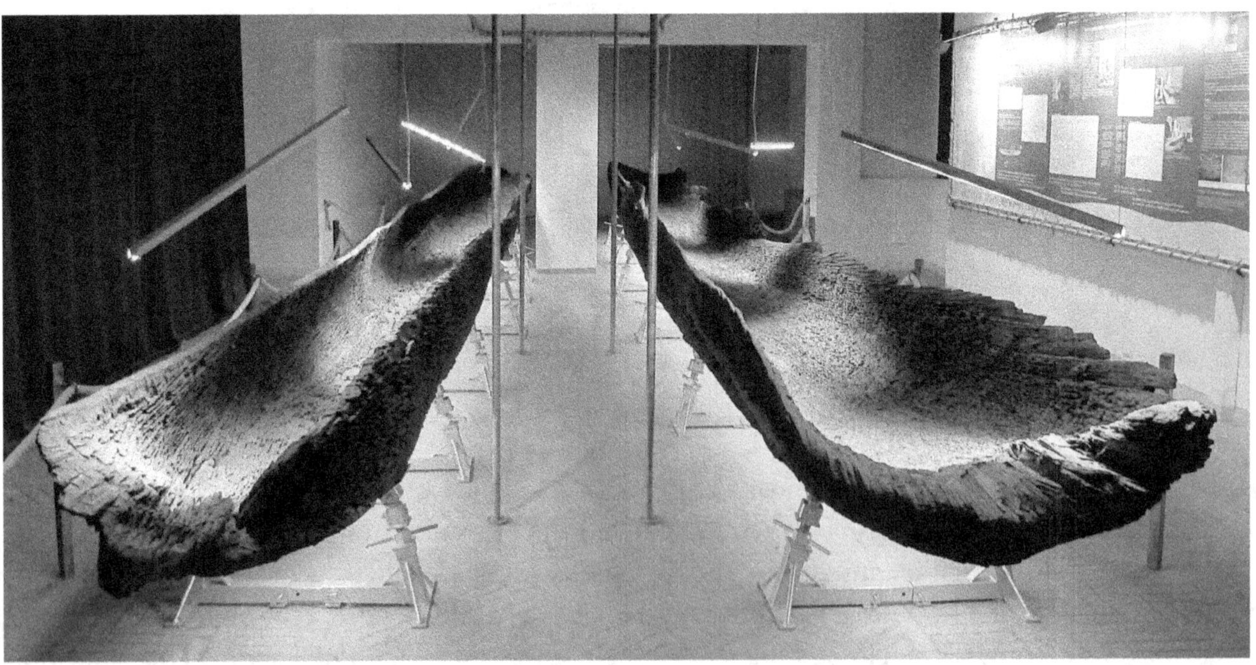

A picture of the remains of Etruscan ships

One of the islands in the Tyrrhenian Sea that Diodorus wrote about was Elba, which is more famous in modern times as the island that Napoleon was initially exiled to in 1814. Elba and the other islands in the Tyrrhenian Sea would remain in the Etruscan sphere of cultural influence until the Romans annexed the territory in 240 BCE (Scarre 1995, 23).

In sum, the Etruscan navy and metals opened Etruria to the rest of the Mediterranean world, and in return the Etruscans were able to utilize styles, techniques, and technologies of other Mediterranean peoples. All of these factors would blend together to form a unique culture.

Etruscan Culture

In terms of culture in the general sense – as the word pertains to art, religion, literature, science, etc. – the flourishing of Etruscan culture began around 900 BCE and lasted for over 500 years (Lorenzi 2010, 36). As noted above, by the 7th century BCE the Villanovan culture had faded and true Etruscan artistic styles began to manifest (Ramage and Ramage 2001, 28). Among the many hallmarks that made Etruscan culture unique and vibrant, art was perhaps the most apparent and enduring, as many aspects of it were carried on by the Romans.

An examination of Etruscan art reveals that although there was a definite Etruscan style, it inherited influences from the Greeks and Phoenicians. The trade between the Etruscans and Phoenicians discussed above not only resulted in the exchange of goods between the two peoples but also the transfer of ideas, particularly in visual arts, from Phoenicia and Carthage to Etruria. The Phoenician influence in Etruscan art can be seen in the many Near Eastern motifs on jars and vases from the 7th century BCE (Grant 1980, 36). The Etruscans were also influenced by Greek artistic styles, but they preferred to employ different iconography in their frescoes and other pictorial depictions. For instance, although the Greeks often depicted hoplite warriors in their art, they rarely showed those warriors engaged in combat and almost never displayed blood or other aspects of graphic violence. The Etruscans on the other hand often rendered vivid images of gladiatorial contests and combat in their art, which has led some scholars to point out that although the Etruscans employed Greek artistic techniques, they "had a special taste for the grisly and eerie." (Grant 1980. 60).

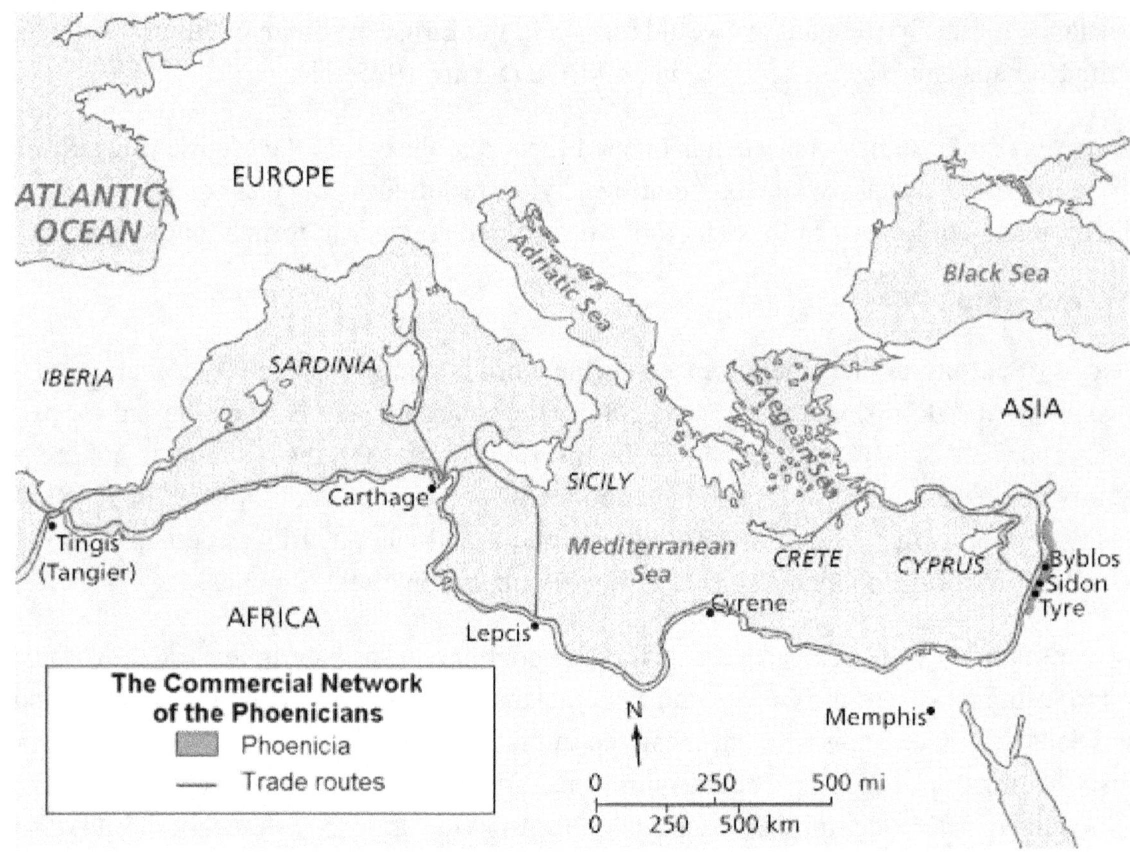

A map of Phoenicia and Phoenician trade routes

Fortunately, even though written sources are scarce, plenty of Etruscan art has survived to provide a glimpse into the Etruscan mind and soul. Perhaps the most indelible of all Etruscan artistic mediums was statuary, as the finished products provide fine example from which previous and contemporary cultures can be compared stylistically. The Etruscans were much like other ancient peoples in that their statues were constructed for utilitarian purposes, usually in a sacred or political context. Etruscan temple statues were often made of terracotta, which is a divergence from the Greeks, and then placed on the roofs of their temples (Ramage and Ramage 2001, 35-36).

Pictures of Etruscan sculptures

Picture of an Etruscan statue depicting a mother and son

Pictures of Etruscan terra cotta

One of the most impressive terracotta temple statues to survive until the modern period is the Apollo of Veii, which is estimated to have been made around 500 BCE and is currently housed in the Museo Nazionale di Villa Giulia in Rome (Ramage and Ramage 2001, 36). The Apollo of Veii bears some stylistic similarities to Greek statuary of the period, but it deviates in important ways. For example, the Apollo is clothed in a toga and shows more movement and life (Ramage and Ramage 2001, 37).

Pictures of the Apollo of Veii

The Etruscans also produced a number of "portrait" sculptures that anticipated Roman portrait sculpture in many ways. Many of the Etruscan portrait sculptures were made of terracotta, like the temple sculptures, but some of the more impressive ones were worked in bronze (Ramage and Ramage 2001, 42). Among the Etruscan bronze statues that clearly influenced later Roman statues is the bearded "Brutus" statue, now housed in the Palazzo dei Conservatori in Rome, and the "Orator," which is in the Archaeological Museum of Florence (Ramage and Ramage 2001, 44). Both statues are of men wearing togas with stoic looks on their faces that are clearly echoed centuries later in Roman Imperial sculptures (Ramage and Ramage 2001, 44).

The Etruscans made excellent statues of human figures that clearly influenced the Romans, but the subject matter of the bronze statues that the Etruscans were most known for was truly unique. Bronze statues were not unique in the ancient world – the ancient Egyptians built statues in bronze and other metals over 1,000 years before the Etruscans (Schäfer 2002, 49) – but the Etruscans introduced a uniquely new iconography of bronze statues: animal statues. Most of the Etruscan bronze animal statues were of mythical creatures, such as the Wounded Chimera, which is currently housed in the Archaeological Museum of Florence (Ramage and Ramage 2001, 38).

The inspiration for the statue may have come from Greek mythology, but the artist imbued the work with purely Etruscan forms.

A picture of an Etruscan chimera statue

The chimera has the body of a lion, a snake for a tail, and a goat head protrudes from its body (Ramage and Ramage 2001, 38). It displays vitality and movement common in Etruscan sculpture as it growls, ready to pounce, and the Wounded Chimera shares some attributes with the most famous of all Etruscan period sculptures: the Capitoline Wolf. The Capitoline Wolf was believed to represent the legendary she-wolf that protected Romulus and Remus from the elements. It is not known for sure if the Capitoline Wolf was ever intended to represent the legendary she-wolf, but throughout centuries people believed it, to the point that two suckling babies were added to the piece during the Renaissance (Ramage and Ramage 2001, 37). Although the Wounded Chimera is more elaborate and projects a more robust image, the Capitoline Wolf is also imbued with a fair amount of life as it stands, apparently growling as a warning to any potential threat.

The Capitoline Wolf

The animal statues represented different aspects of myth and religion, which was also an important aspect of Etruscan culture. Etruscan temples provided a focal point for their culture through the various rituals that were performed in them. The Etruscan city of Veii was home to one of the most important of all their temples, which was dedicated to the god Apollo around 500 BCE (Ramage and Ramage 2001, 32).

Etruscan temple architecture diverged sharply from that of the Greeks and would later provide the template for Roman temple architecture (Ramage and Ramage 2001, 32). The major stylistic difference between Etruscan and Greek temples were the columns on the outside; Greek temples were surrounded by a row of columns, while Etruscan and later Roman temples had two rows of columns that stood in the front (Ramage and Ramage 2001, 32). Etruscan temples also had terracotta statues, as discussed above, placed on their roofs.

A picture of ruins of an Etruscan temple

Pictures of a reconstructed Etruscan temple

Apart from the stylistic difference, Etruscan and Greek temples served the same purpose; they were the holy precinct of a particular deity where devotees would give offerings and perform other important rituals. Unfortunately, not much of the Temple of Veii remains, but its reconstruction by modern scholars, along with some classical accounts, can help recreate an accurate image of Etruscan religion.

In the realm of religion, the Etruscans were known for being particularly devoted to their rituals and myths (Grant 1980, 64). The Etruscans and subsequently the Romans were influenced on certain levels by Greek religion and mythology, and both adopted a number of Greek deities and heroes, such as Heracles and Apollo, while at other times they syncretically merged Greek deities with their own to create uniquely new Etruscan and Roman deities (Cornell 1995, 162). The Greeks also influenced different aspects of religious and mythological iconography in Etruscan art; but despite these similarities and influences, Etruscan religion had many discernible, unique attributes that were practiced for several centuries.

An Etruscan mural depicting Typhon, a monster from Greek mythology

Unlike their Greek contemporaries, Etruscan religion was based on sacred texts, but the nature and number of Etruscan gods remains vague (Grant 1980, 64). Due to the fact that many of those sacred texts are no longer extant, modern scholars are left to reconstruct aspects of Etruscan theology from a combination of classical accounts and modern archaeological research.

One aspect of Etruscan religion that the classical authors wrote extensively about was augury, the practice of interpreting certain things that occur in nature as omens or portents of future events. The practice of augury was actually quite common in the ancient world; for example, the ancient Mesopotamians used astrology to determine omens, the Chinese read them in animal bones, and both the Egyptians and Greeks consulted oracles. Essentially, augury was a method whereby mortals, usually from the priesthood, communicated with the divine for answers concerning temporal questions.

By all accounts, Etruscan augury was quite complicated and involved interpreting bird flights and weather patterns, among other things. Diodorus wrote about Etruscan augury and how the Romans carried on the tradition: "They elaborated the art of divination by thunder and lightning more than all other men; and it is for this reason that the people who rule practically the entire inhabited world show honour to these men even to this day and employ them as interpreters of the omens of Zeus as they appear in thunder and lightning." (Diodorus, *The Library of History*, V, 40, 2).

Augury played such an important role in Etruscan religion that the Romans even followed certain aspects of it, but perhaps the most fundamental and concrete aspect of Etruscan religion that can be observed today is their belief in the afterlife. Indeed, when comparing Greek and Etruscan religious beliefs, perhaps the most visible difference concerns how the two peoples articulated their ideas of the afterlife. The Greeks believed in an afterlife, but it played a small role in their religion and was most apparent in their mythology. Conversely, the Etruscans believed that the afterlife was just a continuation of life in many ways (Grant 1980, 64).

The Etruscan views of the afterlife are best exemplified in their elaborate tombs and funerary sculptures, which depict continuity after death more than a drastic change. Wealthy Etruscans were interred in elaborate tombs, but even the poor made sure to build small, modest tombs (Ramage and Ramage 2001, 30). The more elaborate tombs, such as the "Regolini-Gelassi Tomb" in Cerveteri, were constructed with several chambers that held valuable gold items and contained stone furniture, and the deceased tomb owner's body was placed in a terracotta sarcophagus that often had a life size image of the deceased reclining on the lid (Ramage and Ramage 2001, 39). Although the Romans carried on many of these Etruscan burial traditions, the Etruscans mirrored those of the Near East generally and the Egyptians specifically in many ways (Kyle 2007, 253). The Egyptians are known for building the most elaborate tombs in history, and they were stocked with valuable items and furniture similar to the Etruscan tombs. Although the Greeks did build tombs and mausoleums, some of which were crafted with supreme workmanship, their society as a whole was not as invested in the idea of life after death as the Etruscans were, so elaborate tombs were the exception, not the rule (Obsborne 1998, 218-221).

An Etruscan funerary home

Pictures of Etruscan sarcophagi

Even Strabo noted some similarities between Etruscan and Egyptian religious traditions. In a passage where the geographer described Egyptian temple architecture, he took the time to compare Egyptian temple reliefs with those of the Etruscans: "These are two walls equal in height to the naos, which are at first distant from one another a little more than the breadth of the foundation of the naos, and then, as one proceeds onward, follow converging lines as far as fifty or sixty cubits; and these walls have figures of large images cut in low relief, like the Tyrrhenian images." (Strabo, *Geography*, 17.1, 28).

The historical significance of Etruscan funerary traditions is yet to be determined, but further archaeological, art studies, and comparative religious and historical studies may help determine not only their significance but possibly the origins of the Etruscans.

Religion was certainly at the core of Etruscan culture, but political ideas, namely state formation and expansion, also played a key role. Etruscan political life and government revolved around the concept of the city-state, much like their Greek contemporaries, but few details are known about the precise nature of Etruscan government other than the different cities followed monarchies. That said, there seems to have been some elements of republican government in some of the Etruscan city-states because some republican traditions were passed from the Etruscans to the Romans.

For the most part it appears that the Etruscans practiced a style of government that differed very little from the Romans and most other peoples in the ancient Mediterranean, apart from the Greeks. Although Etruria was the Etruscan homeland, there was never an Etruscan empire or a unified Etruscan state; each Etruscan city pursued its own political agenda (Cornell 1995, 153). Since the Etruscans were never one unified polity then any examination of their government and political structure must be done at the local level by isolating each city. The formation of each Etruscan city followed a similar trajectory, as did Rome's later, which involved the coalescing of villages to create a city (Grant 1980, 17). Numerous factors influenced why villages consolidated into cities: population growth blurred boundaries, trade routes joined villages more closely, and probably most important, cities, especially walled ones, offered better protection against enemies.

Veii was Rome's biggest Etruscan rival since the two were located less than 20 miles from each other, and though Rome had the fortune of being located on the Tiber River, which gave it quick access to the Mediterranean Sea, for hundreds of years Veii was the greater of the two cities. Veii began as a collection of villages located on a plateau that sat above the Tiber River valley (Crawford 2001, 20), but the plateau villages coalesced and formed the city of Veii sometime between 750-700 BCE, and not long after that the city became the dominant cultural and political center in the region (Grant 1980, 221). Rome was the only city to challenge Veii's dominance, and no other city in the region, Etruscan or Latin, came close to either in terms of population or cultural and economic power (Crawford 20001, 20).

Part of Veii's importance was its close proximity to the Tiber River. Although it was not situated directly along the Tiber as Rome was, the river still played an important role in the transport of goods to and from Veii. In fact, the Etruscans of Veii claimed that "Tiber" was the name of one of their kings, and thus they considered the river just as much theirs as it was Rome's (Grant 1980, 231).

In time, Veii became a wealthy city despite its close proximity to Rome. Over the course of several centuries, Veii became wealthy not through trade in metals, as with other Etruscans cities, but through an abundance in agriculture (Grant 1980, 224). As the classical historians described earlier in this report, Veii was in the middle of the fertile zone of Etruria, which meant that not only did it have more than enough food to feed its own citizens, it could also export surpluses for a profit. The Etruscans of Veii would then use the surpluses to invest in cultural edifices, such as the Temple of Apollo (Ramage and Ramage 2001, 32-33).

The Temple of Apollo in Veii was not the only cultural attraction built in the city. In fact, a large portion of the extant works of Etruscan art that are currently in museums have Veii as their provenance, and Veii's reputation as an artistic center in antiquity was apparently well known because the name of one its sculptors, Vulca, has survived (Grant 1980, 224). Since Etruscan artists usually did not "sign" their works, this fact is especially interesting, and it is also historically significant since researchers have been able to search historical records to learn more about Vulca and the cultural life of ancient Veii. Apparently, Vulca's work was in demand throughout Etruria and even in Rome, where he may have owned a workshop (Grant 1980, 224). No doubt there were several other artists like Vulca who are not yet known that made Veii a cultural beacon throughout not just Etruria but all of Italy.

Veii became a cultural center despite its close proximity to Rome, while the city of Tarchnal, better known by the Latin name Tarquinia, grew to prominence less than 100 miles to the northwest (Hencken 1968, 19). Tarquinia was located on the Marta River near the Tyrrehenian Sea and became, politically speaking, the "mother city of Etruria" (Hencken 1968, 18). It was called the mother city of Etruria due to it being one of the oldest and largest Etruscan cities, as well as its central location, which made it the chief city in the Etruscan League for a period (Hencken 1968, 18). As noted earlier, there was never a unified Etruscan state, but the Etruscan cities would form alliances, or leagues, much like other people did in the classical Mediterranean world. For instance, many of the Greek cities formed the Hellenic League to fight the Persians in the early 5th century BCE, and in the late 5th century BCE Athens led the Delian League against Sparta and the Peloponnesian League. Later, in the 3rd century BCE, the Romans led the Latin League against Carthage during the Second Punic War.

Tarquinia's preeminence in the Etruscan League was partially due to being located in the middle of Etruria, but it was also due in part to the city's close proximity to precious metals. Tarquinia is believed to be the first Etruscan city to achieve urbanization, which resulted in it achieving political power much sooner than most of its neighbors (Grant 1980, 20). A consequence of Tarquinia's rise to power, or possibly the reason for it, was its close proximity to the mineral rich Mount Tolfa (Grant 1980, 20). The Etruscans of Tarquinia were able to exploit the metals from Tolfa, which was only 10 miles away, and profit by trading them with the Greeks and Phoenicians, while also forging weapons to keep the Etruscan League in line.

Tarquinia's power peaked in the 7th century BCE and is marked by elaborate tombs that were adorned with precious items from as far away as Phoenicia and Egypt (Grant 1980, 125). Although not directly on the sea, Tarquinia's proximity to the Marta River helped facilitate some trade, and it also exerted direct influence over the coast (Grant 1980, 130-131).

Despite Tarquinia's prime position in Etruria, its dominance in the region only lasted a little over a century before it was eclipsed by other cities, most notably Veii, in the 6th century BCE. Eventually another Etruscan city, Cisra (modern Cerveteri), took control of the mines and Tarquinia's dominance ended (Grant 1980, 24). Although Tarquinia lost its dominance over the other Etruscan cities it continued to be an important center until the Romans conquered it in the 3rd century BCE (Hencken 1968, 20).

A picture of the murals on a tomb in Tarquinia

A New City

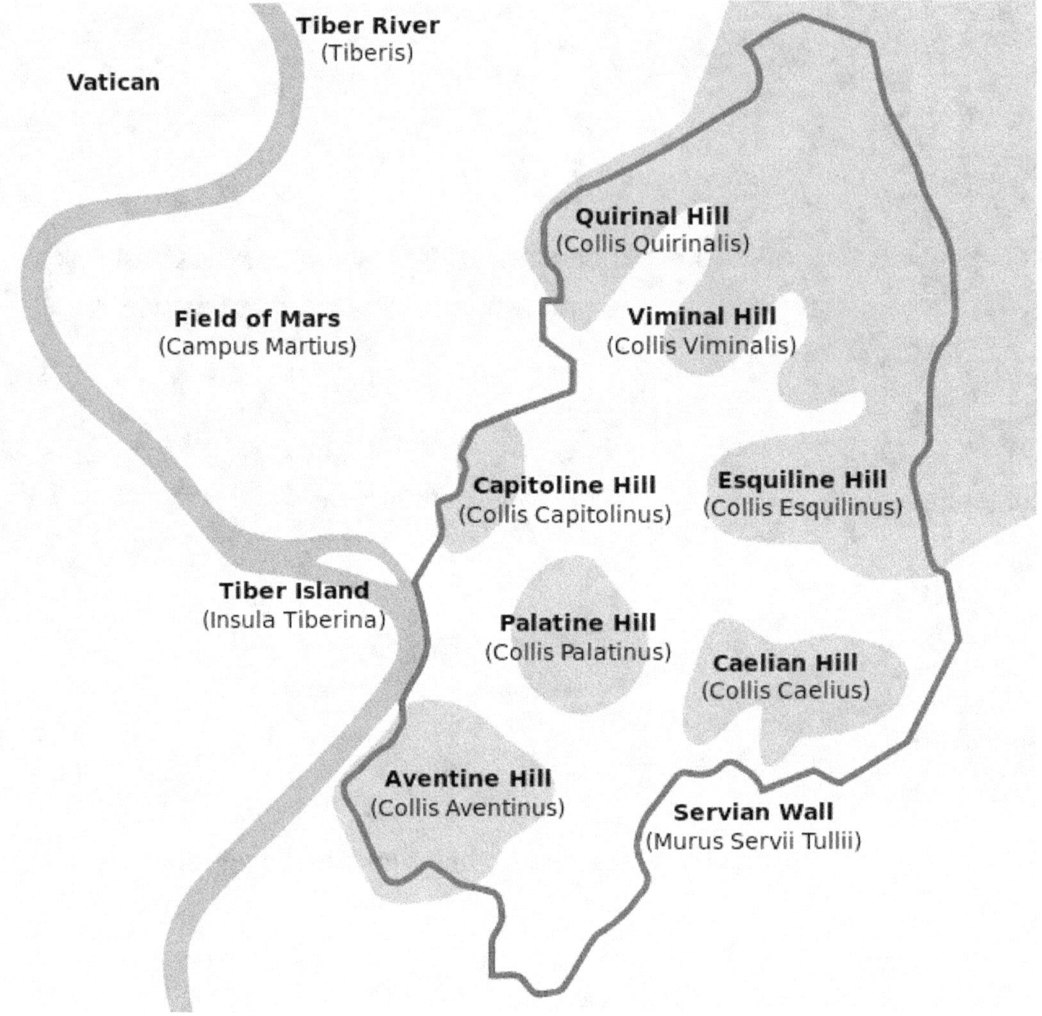

A map of the hills

"The populace like the sea is motionless in itself, but stirred by every wind, even the slightest breeze." – Livy, 1st century BCE historian

An assortment of Italic tribes had been occupying the boot of Italy long before the rise of the Romans. The bulk of these people hailed from the lands north of the Adriatic Sea, gradually moving in to the unoccupied nooks and crannies of the peninsula over the years. A fraction were Greek nomads who sailed from their motherland, docking by the shores of southern Italy. Historians described these tribes as primitive and "scarcely civilized," but these settlers, who relied mostly on their flock, would become the very first to crack into the rough earth of never-before-cultivated Italian soil. For the most part, these tribes rarely strayed from familiar territory, for conversing with one another was another struggle in itself; each spoke a crude blend of Aryan and Indo-European languages.

4 tribes composed of what is now referred to as the "Italic race" made up the majority of the population – the Latins, the Sabellians, the Oscans, and the Umbri. The Latins were predominantly in central Italy, living in villages throughout and encircling the Old Latium region, which sat between Mount Circeo and the Tiber River, as early as the late Bronze Age (1200-900 BCE). Latin villagers lived in clusters of "straw-thatched" huts, which later expanded to settlements on the Alban Hills southeast of Rome. When the city erected defensive walls in later years, many of these villages blossomed into cities, bound together by a common language and their worship for Jupiter, the supreme Roman god of light and sky.

The Sabellians, often depicted as a fierce and warmongering people, lived to the south and east of their Latin and Oscan neighbors by the Appenine Range. Since green thumbs were a rarity among the Sabellians, the villagers banked on their livestock, or the booty obtained from looting the harvests of nearby villages for sustenance.

The Oscans, who inhabited the lands southward of the Old Latium, were also quick to grab their spears. They shared many customs with the Latin tribes, but lagged a step behind when it came to agricultural methods, technological innovations, and the general advancement of their society. Many of their descendants, such as the Volscians, Aequians, and Hernicans, would later engage skirmishes with the Romans.

The Umbri were supposedly the oldest of all Italic tribes. The spelling of the original name, "*Ombrii*," which translates to the "people of the thunderstorm," was given to them by the Greeks, for the Umbri were believed to have survived the "Deluge," their take on the divine flood. Umbri communities constructed some of the land's first temples in rural areas, devvoted to Minerva, Clitumnus, Feronia, and other Umbrian deities. The Eugubian Tablets, recovered centuries later, revealed carvings written in the ancient Umbrian language that hinted at animal sacrifices and other early religious rituals. Despite their seniority over the tribes, they would become overwhelmed during later Roman invasions, and either broke up into even smaller villages or merged with nearby communities.

Much of the birth and development of early Rome, however, is indebted to the Etruscans, who descended upon and captured the walled Italic cities of Rome midway through the 7th century BCE, taking the constellation of unrefined clay huts with patchy straw roofs and marrying them to create a unified city.

It would only be a matter of time before Roman civilization, which bordered Etruscan territory, absorbed its culture. To begin with, Roman religion, much like that of the Etruscans, revolved around an array of gods and goddesses who could be swayed into interfering with human affairs through sacrifice and other religious rituals. Roman pagans themselves more than dabbled in augury; their priests also possessed sacred texts disclosed to them by the gods and Etruscan sages.

The Etruscan language is also considered an ancestor of the Latin tongue. In fact, Latin has lifted quite a few words straight out of the Etruscan books, such as *"fasces,"* a weapon carried by magisterial attendants featuring an ax blade projecting from a bundle of elmwood, and the *"toga palmata,"* a magistrate's robe. Wealthy Romans of the time understood the significance of Etruscan education and enrolled their children in both Etruscan and Greek institutes.

Etruscan culture would also leave its enduring imprints on the societal and Christian cultures of Rome. Gladiators brawling until only one was left standing during the funerals for Etruscan nobles was a custom that would later become one of the most distinguishable earmarks of ancient Roman tradition. Depictions of Christian demons and fallen angels were said to have resembled Etruscan demons, and early Roman art and literature were also said to have been heavily seasoned with Etruscan elements.

Some of the most pivotal parts of the Etruscan influence on Roman civilization were their impact on the infrastructure of the villages, as well as the molding of the Roman governing system and its political values. Before the arrival of the Etruscans, the major settlements on the seven hills of Rome – the Palatine, Aventine, Campidoglio, Esquiline, Quirinal, Viminal, and Caelian Hills – were cordoned off by their borders and conflicting customs, and as a result, mostly kept to themselves. That was, until the Etruscans introduced an annual region-wide festival that would bring the previously hesitant inhabitants of all hills together.

The *Septimontium* was not only the name of the complex of villages sprinkled throughout the seven *"montes,"* it also referred to the religious festival all the villagers participated in. Due to the time frame, little information has survived about these celebrations. Chroniclers believe the villagers gathered to pay homage to Apollo, the "Laurel-bearing sun god" with chariot races, plays, and sacred tokens of the people's gratitude. Following an animated procession enlivened by singing, dancing, and other forms of merriment around the Palatine and Esquiline Hills, the villagers convened at the former hill for a special sacrifice. Authorities cleared out large sections of the streets and forbade the use of chariots and other vehicles to make room for the procession. The sacrifice, known as a *"palatuar,"* was conducted by a "bare-headed" pagan priest they called the *"flamen palatualis."*

Offering "sparkling grains of pure salt" and the "mate of a woolly ewe" slain and neatly gutted by the sacrificial butcher *(agones),* as well as other symbolic gifts, the villagers hoped for blessings of good weather and bountiful harvests from the gods. Other reports of gifts given include gilded statues, such as an ox and a pair of goats for Apollo, and a heifer for Apollo's mother, Leto. Afterwards, some Roman emperors presented senators and knights with baskets brimming with loaves of bread and hunks of meat; miniature versions of these baskets were also doled out to the masses. The festival of the *Septimontium* would become a staple pagan festival that Roman Christians would later adamantly refuse to partake in.

Arguably the most successful of the *Septimontium* team-building activities were the series of games developed especially for the festival, known as the "*Ludi Apollinares,*" or the "Apollo Games." These games were said to have been paid for through taxes acquired from village treasuries, and donations fished from the public. These games took up the majority of the festival's repertoire. They included the *Ludi Scaenici,* a collection of religious plays, mimes, and dances dedicated to the sun gods, the *Ludi Circenses,* the spirited chariot races (later held in the Circus Maximus), and running races, wrestling matches, and other recreational tests of skill. Livy, a Roman historian from the 1ˢᵗ century BCE, summed up the bustling atmosphere of the *Septimontium* festival: "All the people took part in them [wore] wreaths of flowers. The married women offered prayers. The doors to the houses were opened, meals eaten in the open, and the day marked with every observance..."

It was supposedly through the *Septimontium* that the villages on the hills learned to work as a cohesive unit. The villagers collaborated to drain the low-lying marshy grounds between the hills to the best of their abilities. They transformed these uninhabitable and "malarial" lands into markets where all the villagers could trade, which only strengthened the trust and new political bridges built between these villages. Through the guidance of the Etruscan elite, which instilled in them the concept of a monarchy and the tools to build this centralized form of government, the scattered villages of Rome were soon compressed into one city.

Rome emerged as an official city-state of its own under Etruscan rule. They were buttressed by an initially modest, but soon-to-be stellar military, with much of the training and battle techniques passed onto them by the Etruscans. During spells of strife and dances with disaster, the villagers, now citizens under the same government, learned to pool their resources together to aid their fellow countrymen.

The Etruscans are also credited with planting the seeds for what Rome would become most recognizable for: the structurally sound and phenomenal urban infrastructure seemingly eons ahead of its time. The city's aqueducts, underground sewer system, public baths, smooth stone roads, and durable bridges were said to have been modeled after Etruscan blueprints. The Etruscans also helped to boost Roman trade, and discovered ways to enhance the fields of agriculture and the local metal production.

By the 5ᵗʰ century BCE, Rome had landed on the map as one of the mightiest and most influential cities in all of Old Latium, and ironically, all the assistance and resources the Etruscans had parted with would ultimately contribute to their own demise. The Roman armies grew more potent and were soon assertive enough to conquer the last of its neighbors, thereby enlarging the republic.

Once they had triumphed in convincing the Latin villagers to revolt against its leaders and join forces with the republic, the Romans would be able to take on the Etruscans, whom historians say "lacked a strong national identity." As enterprising as the Etruscans were, those envious of them found a crucial flaw in the disorganization of the multiple governments within Etruria.

Some cities were guarded by scores of soldiers, but a large chunk of them were untrained and barely older than the armors on their bodies. While other Etruscan cities had managed to get their hands on veteran troops, they were outnumbered by Greek and Roman soldiers, many of the latter trained by the Etruscan veterans themselves.

War

The conflicts between the Etruscans and Romans are well documented by classical historians, but unfortunately there are inherent problems with those accounts. As always with the classical accounts, there was a certain amount of hyperbole and invective against the group deemed foreign, which in this case was the Etruscans. Ancient historians were often under pressure by the ruling class, whether they were part of an empire or republic, to produce a narrative that was friendly to the ruling powers, which naturally influenced the narratives that they wrote and the information that historians have received (Marincola 2004, 86-87). Moreover, many of the classical accounts concerning the conflicts between the Etruscans and Romans don't include dates, so it's necessary to reconstruct chronologies that may not always be precise.

Nonetheless, a general outline of the events can be gleaned, and the overall picture is an essentially one sided affair. The Etruscans, usually led by Veii, would resist Roman expansion, but they lost most of the major battles. Archaeological evidence suggests that the Etruscans expanded their influence south of Etruria into the Campania region of Italy sometime around 600 BCE, and since Campania is south of the Latium region, which Rome is in, some believe that the Etruscans controlled that region for a time as well (Cornell 1995, 154-55).

Although there is obvious logic to this argument, there is no evidence, other than the Tarquins who ruled Rome, to suggest that the Etruscans ever dominated Latium, and the very nature of Etruscan rule in Campania is problematic in itself. There is no evidence to suggest that the Etruscans ever invaded the region with armies; instead, the signs seem to indicate that a process of Etruscan emigration to Campania resulted in an Etruscan elite class ruling the region (Cornell 1995, 155). One only has to look at how this pattern took place in Rome to see how it was possible. There, the Etruscans came to Rome peacefully and established a political dynasty that married in with the local elites, and the same thing is probably what happened in Campania, though without more evidence it is difficult to say for sure at this point.

If anything, it seems that when the Romans and Etruscans finally came into conflict, the Etruscans were not a passive party and were quite possibly the aggressor at times. According to the classical sources, the conflicts between the Etruscans and Rome began in the period under the semi-mythical first ruler of Rome, Romulus, and continued off and on until the Etruscan city of Volsinii was destroyed in 264 BCE, which put Etruria effectively under Roman control (Cornell 1995, 45). Due to their close proximity, Veii and Rome clashed a number of times, especially after the Roman Republic was established in 509 BCE (Grant 1980, 231).

The causes of the conflicts between the Etruscans and Roman were usually political and economic. It may be surprising, but ethnic considerations had little to do with the tensions between the two peoples. One of the particular points of contention was the Etruscan city of Fidenae, which both cities claimed.

Livy dated one of the first wars between Veii and Rome back to the reign of Romulus and described what happened: "The war fever soon spread to Veii, which, like Fidenae, was an Etruscan town. It was also a close neighbor of Rome, and the danger of such propinquity in the event of Rome proving hostile to all her neighboring communities was a further exacerbation. . . In the fight which ensued Romulus used no strategy; the sheer power of his veteran troops sufficed for victory, and he pursued the retreating enemy to the walls of Veii. The town itself was strongly fortified and well sited for defence; Romulus, accordingly, made no attempt to take it, but contented himself on the return march with wasting the cultivated land, more by way of revenge than for what he could take from it. The loss the Veientes suffered from the devastation did as much as their defeat in the field to secure their submission and they sent envoys to Rome to treat for peace." (Livy, *The Early History of Rome*, 1.15).

Livy was no general, so he failed to realize the tactical importance of the Romans' scorched earth policy in Etruria. The Romans no doubt knew how fertile the region around Veii was, and that the Etruscan city depended on the crops not only for food but also for trade. Thus, by destroying them, the Romans forced the Etruscans of Veii to the negotiating table.

Despite the destruction and defeat, Veii quickly rebounded and once more challenged Rome for authority in the region. During the reign of the Roman king Tullus Hostilus (673-642 BCE), Veii and Rome once more went to war, this time with the city of Fidenae at the center of the events. Apparently the Etruscans hoped to entice the Latin city of Alba, which had been subjugated by the Romans, to join their war against Rome, but the Etruscans badly miscalculated with the Albans and it led to a disastrous defeat. Livy wrote, "The people of Fidenae, a colony of Rome, were induced in concert with Veii to declare war by a promise that Alba would join them. . . The Roman troops who had been in touch with the Albans and now found their flank exposed were at a loss to account for their withdrawal; then a messenger galloped up to the king with the report that the Alban army was deserting. . . Tullus' loud assertion had been audible enough, and most of the Fidenates understood Latin as emigrants from Rome had settled amongst them in the past. They accordingly beat a retreat, to obviate the danger of being cut off from home by a sudden descent of the Albans from the hills. Tullus attacked, made short work of the Fidenates on the wing, and then turned with increased fury on the Veientians, who were already shaken by their friends' discomfiture. Their resistance broke and they fled in disorder to the river in their rear." (Livy, *The Early History of Rome*, 1.27).

Although Rome claimed victory in its first few wars with Veii, the victories were for the most part inconclusive and Veii continued to be a threat. At the same time, the leaders of Veii realized that they could not defeat Rome alone, so they turned to a new strategy.

The course of the wars between the Etruscans and Romans took a turn during the reigns of the two Roman kings known collectively as the Tarquins. The Tarquins were two kings who were ironically of Etruscan origin, but in their dealings with the lands of their ancestors they showed no mercy. The classical authors generally do not distinguish between Lucius Tarquius Priscus (616-579 BCE) and Lucius Tarquinius Superbus (535-509 BCE), so some confusion about the events is apparent in the accounts. According to Dionysius, the Etruscans of Veii reorganized the Etruscan League after Tarquin and the Romans defeated their Latin neighbors, the Sabines. "The Sabines, subdued by this calamity, grew sensible of their own weakness, and sending ambassadors, concluded a truce from the war for six years. But the Tyrrhenians, angered not only because they had been often defeated by the Romans, but also because Tarquinius had refused to restore to them the prisoners he held when they sent an embassy to demand them, but retained them as hostages, passed a vote that all the Tyrrhenian cities should carry on the war jointly against the Romans . . . But King Tarquinius, having for the ensuing year armed all the Romans and taken as many troops as he could get from his allies, led them out against the enemy at the beginning of spring, before the Tyrrehnians could be assembled from all their cities and march against him as they had done before. . . The army of Romans, commanded by Tarquinius, laid waste and ravaged the country of the Veientes and carried off much booty, and when numerous reinforcements assembled from all the Tyrrhenian cities to aid the Veientes, the Romans engaged them in battle and gained an incontestable victory." (Dionysius of Halicarnassus, *The Antiquities of Rome*, III, 57, 1-5).

Although the Etruscans were handed yet another defeat by the Romans, they persevered and continued to be a thorn in their neighbor's side. Once the Sabines were defeated, the Tarquins of Rome were free to focus their aggression towards Etruria, and a new round of warfare erupted between the Etruscans and Romans that lasted for three years, this time threatening to be the demise of both peoples. The king of Roman realized that the Etruscans were not his only enemies and thus decided to show a level of magnanimity in ending the war when he delivered a speech to the Etruscans that demonstrated his benevolence. Dionysius quoted the Roman leader: "Hear now upon what fair terms I am granting you. I am not eager to put any of the Tyrrhenians to death or to banish any from their country or to punish any with the loss of their possessions. I impose no garrisons or tributes upon any of your cities, but permit each of them to enjoy its own laws and its ancient form of government. But it granting you this I thing I ought to obtain one thing from you in return for all that I am giving, and that is the sovereignty over your cities – something that I shall possess even against your will as long as I am powerful in arms, though I prefer to obtain it with your consent rather than without it." (Dionysius of Halicarnassus, *The Antiquities of Rome*, III, 59, 2-3).

Of course, Tarquinius probably had other motives besides magnanimity for his peace proposal that should be considered. The Etruscans presented numerous problems to Roman expansion, but they were a power that Rome could not defeat in the years before the Republic, so peace treaties took the place of conquest. The Romans also had to protect their flank as other Latin peoples to their south and west continually gave them problems.

As Rome made the transition from monarchy to republic, it actually became more aggressive and expansionistic. The first century and a half of the Roman Republic was marked by the Romans reasserting their authority over other Latins, such as the Sabines, and expanding into other Italic peoples' lands, such as the Samnites and Umbrians (Crawford 2001, 26). While most of this expansion was to Rome's east and south, hostilities with the Etruscans were renewed to the north, and at the center of the conflict was the city of Veii once again.

A new war between Veii and Rome took place from 476-475 BCE and set into motion the former's eventual collapse and the latter's hegemony over the Italian peninsula. The accounts of both Livy and Dionysius relate that the Roman consul, Vlerius, led the campaign against the Etruscans. Livy wrote that the Etruscans of Veii were able to induce the Latin Sabines to join their cause: "But war broke out again with the Veientes, now in alliance with the Sabines. The consul Valerius was dispatched to Veii with an army reinforced by contingents from the Latins and Hernici, and with no time wasted led an assault upon the Sabines, who had taken up a position just beyond the walls of the town. The attack was a surprise and completely disorganized the defence; and while small scattered groups were trying ineffectually to deal with it, Valerius got possession of the gate which had been his first objective." (Livy, *The Early History of Rome*, 2.53)

Dionysius' account is similar to Livy's but adds some more details, particularly about the disorganized Etruscan retreat: "Not long afterwards an army of the Romans marched out against the Tyrrhenians under the command of Publius Valerius, one of the consuls. For the forces of the Veientes had again assembled and had been joined by the Sabines. . . At last the Tyrrhenians, forced by the Roman horse, gave way and retired to their camp. The consul followed, and when he came near their ramparts – these had been poorly constructed and the place, as I said, was not very secure – he attacked them in many places at once, continuing his exhausting efforts all the rest of that day and not even resting the following night. The Tyrrhenians, exhausted by their continual hardships, left their camp at break of day, some fleeing to their city and others dispersing themselves in the neighboring woods." (Dionysius of Halicarnassus, *The Antiquities of Rome*, IX, 35, 1-3).

Once again the Etruscans were soundly defeated on the battlefield by the Romans, but as with all of the previous wars, the Romans were unable to permanently subdue Veii. Livy wrote that the consuls succeeding Valerius were forced to grant Veii another peace: "The next consuls to take office were Lucius Furius and Gaius Manlius; the latter had Veii as his sphere of action, but there were no hostilities as a forty years' truce was granted at Veii's request, on condition of their paying a cash indemnity and supplying Rome with grain." (Livy, *The Early History of Rome*, 2.53).

Interestingly, the peace between Veii and Rome lasted almost 40 years, but it was broken around 437 BCE when the two cities quarreled once more over Fidenae. As hostilities reemerged between Veii and Rome in 437, Veii was led into battle personally by its king, Tolumnius, and the Etruscans also enjoyed a numerical superiority in the battle according to Livy. The historian wrote, "The Veientes, who were numerically strong, sent a detachment round the back of the hills to attack the Roman camp during the coming engagement, the main body of their force holding the right of the allied armies, with the contingent from Falerii on the left and that from Fidenae in the centre; on the Roman side, the Dictator commanded the right, and Capitolinus the left, while the Master of Horse led out his squadrons in front of the center. . . The weight of both attacks was tremendous and in no part of their line could the Etruscans stand against them; the Etruscan horse offered the stiffest resistance, and of all their mounted troops none fought with such courage as Tolumnius the king, who kept the fight going by repeated individual attacks upon Roman cavalrymen as they galloped in loose order in pursuit of the fugitives. . .The blow struck home and Tolumnius fell; instantly, Cossus dismounted and as Tolumnius struggled to rise struck him down again with the boss of his shield and with repeated thrusts of his spear finally pinned him to the ground. Then he stripped the lifeless body of its armour, cut off its head and, sticking it on the point of a lance, returned to the fight with his spoils. At the sight of their dead king the enemy broke and fled. That ended the resistance of the Etruscan cavalry, which had been the only arm to keep the issue in doubt." (Livy, *The Early History of Rome*, 4.18-4.20).

The death of Veii's king was a turning point in the conflicts between the Etruscans and Rome. Before Tolumnius was killed, the Etruscans were able to rebound from their battlefield losses against the Romans, but after the defeat in 437, Etruria was doomed to become Roman territory. Sometime in 435 or 425 BCE – modern researchers are divided over the exact date (Grant 1980, 232) – Fidenae was finally seized by the Romans; but the Etruscans still had enough power to unite once more against their traditional enemy. Veii once more led the Etruscan League, but at this time the alliance was feeble and ultimately stymied by a lack of direction and vision from its members. Livy explained, "The capture of Fidenae caused great alarm in Etruria, especially in the towns of Veii and Falerii – the former from dread of a similar fate, and the latter from the uneasy consciousness of having supported Fidenae when the war started, even though in the second outbreak she had stood aside. Accordingly when these two communities obtained the consent of the Twelve Towns for a general council of all Etruria to meet at the temple of Voltumna, the Senate in Rome expected a serious rising, and to meet it, decreed that Mamercus Postumius Tubertus Master of the Horse, and the danger from a united Etruria being so much greater than last time, when only Veii and Fidenae were involved, mobilization began on a proportionately greater scale. . . War plans were discussed in the councils of the Volscians and Aequians, and also in Etruria at the shrine of Voltumna, where a decision was postponed for a year and a decree issued forbidding any further meeting until the years was over, in spite of the urgent and bitter representations of Veii that she was threatened with the same disaster as that which had brought destruction to Fidenae." (Livy. *The Early History of Rome*, 4.24-4.25). The feeble Etruscan League was not able to stop further Roman expansion into Etruria, but Veii was able to hold on to its independence for two more decades.

As the 5th century BCE came to a close, Veii and the Etruscans became an anachronism; they were a venerable but ancient culture whose time was past, and they seemed to hold up the progress that the Romans were attempting to bring with them to the rest of Italy. The final war between Rome and Veii began at the end of the century, which would be unlike all of the other wars between the two great cities and would end in the total destruction of Veii. The Romans besieged Veii for 10 years before they were able to breach its walls in 396 BCE. Livy described the combat: "Defeat of the enemy in the field was crowned by the capture of his camp; a mass of valuable material was taken, most of which was given for disposal to the quaestor, only a small proportion being distributed amongst the men. The army then proceeded to Veii, where Camillus increased the number of redoubts and by giving out that no one was to fight without orders put a stop between the town walls and the Roman stockade. The men who had been employing themselves in this way were turned on to digging. Of the digging operations, by far the most important and laborious was the construction of a tunnel to lead up into the central fortress of the town; this work was now begun, and to keep it going without intermission the men engaged upon it were divided into six parties, working six hours each in rotation. . . From every direction and with overwhelming numbers Roman troops moved forward to the assault, to distract attention from the more imminent danger from the tunnel. . . In readiness for the decisive stroke the tunnel had been filled with picked men, and now, without warning, it discharged them into the temple of Juno on the citadel. The enemy, who were manning the walls against the threat from outside, were attacked from behind; bolts were wrenched off the gates; buildings were set on fire as women and slaves on the roof flung stones and tiles at the assailants. A fearful din arose: yells of triumph, shrieks of terror, wailing of women, and the pitiful crying of children; in an instant of time the defenders were flung from the walls and the town gates opened; Roman troops came pouring through, or climbed the now defenceless walls; everything was overrun, in every street the battle raged. After terrible slaughter resistance began to slacken, and Camillus gave the order to spare all who were not carrying arms." (Livy, *The Early History of Rome*, 5.20-21).

With Veii's destruction, there was no other city capable of leading the Etruscan League. By 310 BCE, when the Romans made their final thrust into Etruria, they did so uncontested for the most part (Crawford 2001, 482). After the Roman annexation and conquest of Etruria, the Etruscan people lingered in a sort of political limbo until Roman citizenship was extended to them in 90 BCE (Lorenzi 2010, 39).

The Romans may have been the ultimate victors in the struggle for hegemony over the Italian peninsula, but the Etruscan influence continued to resonate for centuries. The degree to which the Etruscans had influence on Roman is debated by academics, but the fact that they did influence many Roman traditions is not.

Some scholars, such as T.J. Cornell, argue that since little to no Etruscan linguistic and literary influences can be detected in Roman culture (157), among other notable differences, then the overall Etruscan influence on Rome was minimal (172). In some ways, Cornell is correct, as many of the influences are relatively minor; but when they are considered in their totality, then a more complete picture emerges, and it demonstrates the Etruscan influences upon Rome were widespread if not always deep.

One of the more interesting and somewhat ironic influences the Etruscans had on early Roman history was the Tarquin Dynasty itself, which ruled Rome until the inception of the Republic. As the fighting indicated, the Tarquins ruled as Romans and were more than willing to fight the Etruscans, but an examination of the sources reveals that their origins were firmly in Etruria. Tradition portrays pre-Republican Rome as a primarily Latin city but one that accepted outsiders, such as the Sabines and the Etruscans (Cornell 1995, 157). Two Sabines ruled Rome before the Tarquins did, which gave the city a cosmopolitan composition (Cornell 1995, 157). In many ways Rome was the New York City of its time, a place where people could go to find better fortunes that were not available elsewhere. This attitude is demonstrated in Livy's account concerning how the first Tarquin rose to power in Rome: "A man named Lucumo left Tarquinii where he was born and came to settle in Rome. He was ambitious and wealthy and hoped to rise to a position of eminence there, such as his native town was never likely to afford him; for though born at Tarquinii he was by blood an alien, being the son of Demaratus of Corninth. . . His self-confidence was further increased by his marriage to Tanaquil, an aristocratic young woman who was not of a sort to put up with humbler circumstances in her married life than those she had been previously accustomed to. The Etruscans of Tarquinii despised Lucumo as the son of a foreign refugees, and to Tanquil the indignity of his position soon became intolerable. . . Rome was a young and rising community; there would be opportunities for an active and courageous man in a place where all advancement came swiftly and depended upon ability. After all, King Tatius had been a foreigner –a Sabine; Numa had been called to the throne form his native Cures. . . Thus dreaming upon future greatness, Lucumo and Tanquil drove into Rome, where they bought a house, and Lucumo took the name Lucius Tarquinius Priscus." (Livy, *The Early History of Rome*, 1.33-1.34). Once Tarquin and Tanaquil established their home in Rome, it was not long before the Greek-Etruscan rose in Roman society to eventually become the king.

At this point, Rome was technically a monarchy, but the government contained some elements of popular rule that were introduced by the Tarquins. According to Livy, Tarquin introduced the concept of political campaigning to Rome. " Tarquin (as we shall now call Lucumo), was anxious that the election of a successor to the throne should be held at the earliest possible moment. A date was announced, and a few days before it Tarquin sent the two boys out of town on a hunting expedition. He is said to have been the first to canvass personally for votes, and to have delivered a public speech designed to win public support." (Livy, *The Early History of Rome*, 1.34). It is unknown if Tarquin learned the ideas of political campaigning and oratory in Etruria or if he invented those concepts, but Livy's account unequivocally states that the Etruscan-Roman king was the first person to use them in Rome.

The Tarquins are also credited with establishing some of the monuments and points of interest that have come to be associated with Roman culture. According to Livy, after the first Tarquins' first military victory, he publicly celebrated the occasion by having public games and the construction of government buildings. The historian wrote, "He celebrated public games on a scale more elaborate and opulent than any of his predecessors. It was on this occasion that our Circus Maximus was originally planned. On the ground marked out for it special places were assigned to Senators and knights to erect their stands in – or 'decks' as they were called. These stands were supported on props and raised twelve feet from the ground. Horses and boxers, mostly from Etruria, provided the entertainment." (Livy, *The Early History of Rome,* 1.36).

A mural in an Etruscan tomb depicting boxers

The spirit of civic involvement that the Romans are known for was then at least partially influenced by the Etruscans, but the passage also relates the Etruscan influence on Roman sports and entertainment. The Romans are known for staging a number of public sporting events and competitions, of which gladiatorial combat is the best known, but an examination of Roman sports reveals that although they derived some influences from the Greeks, Roman ideals of sport and spectacle diverged in many ways, and this may be attributed to an Etruscan influence. Two notable sporting ideals that the Romans and Etruscans shared that differed markedly from the Greeks were the avoidance of nudity in competition and the idea that respectable members of society were spectators, not competitors (Kyle 2007, 256). Gladiatorial combat was also never practiced by the Greeks, but it was by both the Etruscans and Romans.

Few accounts of Etruscan gladiatorial events are known, but an account from Herodotus describes an incident that comes very close. The event concerns a Etruscan military victory over the Phocaeans, after which the Etruscans decided to use the Phocaean prisoners for target practice. Herodotus wrote, "The Carthaginians and Tyrrhenians drew lots for the possession of the prisoners from the ships which were sunk. Of the Tyrrhenians, the people of Agylla got by far the largest number, and they took them all ashore and stoned them to death." (Herodotus, *The Histories*, I, 167). Other evidence for Etruscan gladiatorial style games includes a 6th century tomb painting that depicts a blindfolded man with a club being attacked by a dog (Kyle 2007, 270-271). The idea of mutual, one-on-one style gladiatorial combat may have originated in Rome, but public executions and animal combat/hunts probably emanated from the Etruscans (Kyle 2007, 271).

A fresco depicting Etruscan gladiators

The Etruscans clearly influenced some aspects of Roman sport and public entertainment, and their influence can also be seen in several aspects of the style and rituals that were common in public displays of government during both the Republican and Imperial periods. One of the primary things that set the Romans apart from other ancient peoples was their method of government, and among the things that made Roman government unique was its style, particularly the many rituals that accompanied it. The numerous rituals and symbols that were inherent in ancient Roman government make it seem a bit arcane and esoteric, but most of it was quite logical and borrowed from the Etruscans. The bundle of sticks tied together with an axe head (known as the *fasces*), along with the toga and royal purple robes, were all inherited from the Etruscans. Diodorus noted, "They were also the authors of that dignity which surrounds rulers providing their rulers with lictors and an ivory stool and a toga with a purple band; and in connection with their houses they invented the peristyle, a useful device for avoiding the confusion connected with attending throngs; and these things were adopted for the most part by the Romans, who added to their embellishment and transferred them to their own political institutions." (Diodorus, *The Library of History*, V, 40, 1-2).

According to Dionysius, Etruscan ambassadors also introduced the legendary eagle standards to the Romans: "The ambassadors, having received this answer, departed, and after a few days returned, not merely with words alone, but bringing the insignia of sovereignty with which they used to decorate their own kings. These were a crown of gold, and ivory throne, a scepter with an eagle perched on its head, a purple tunic decorated with gold, and an embroidered purple robe like those the kings of Lydia and Persia used to wear, except that it was not rectangular in shape like theirs, but semicircular." (Dionysius, *The Antiquities of Rome*, III, 61. 1).

Perhaps the most profound influence had on Roman was augury. Etruscan augury impressed the Romans so much that they employed Etruscan priests to read omens, but they also learned the practice themselves. According to Strabo, augury was more widespread before the Romans dominated the Mediterranean, but they carried on the Etruscan traditions to a certain extent while ignoring other forms of well-known augury such as the Egyptian oracle of Amun: "Among the ancients both divination in general and oracles were held in greater honour, but now great neglect of them prevails, since the Romans are satisfied with the oracles of Sibylla, and with the Tyrrhenian prophecies obtained by means of the entrails of animals, flight of birds, and omens from the sky; and on this account, also, the oracle of Ammon has been almost abandoned, though it was held in honour in earlier times." (Strabo, *Geography*, 17.1, 43). Augury continued to play an important role in Roman culture well into the Christian period.

Another religious influence that the Etruscans imparted to the Romans was the idea of a calendar and many of the names of the month (Hoenigswald 1941, 202). Although some month names were obviously latter added to the "Julian Calendar" – July and August are named for Julius Caesar and Augustus respectively – the original calendar came from the Etruscans. The Etruscan calendar, like most ancient calendars, was primarily established to ensure the proper celebration of religious festivals.

The Romans apparently also admired cultic aspects of Etruscan religion. The Roman god of war, Mars, and his priesthood is thought to be one of the most quintessential aspects of Roman religion because the Romans were such ardent believers in the benefits of warfare. Although Mars may have had Roman origins and was based on the Greek Ares, his priesthood, known as the Salian order, was an Etruscan institution (Grant 1980, 230).

The Romans also invited the Etruscan sculptor Vulca, who was discussed previously, to Rome in order to make the statue of Jupiter that stood at their temple dedicated to Jupiter, Juno, and Minerva (Grant 1980, 230). The religious statues that Vulca was commissioned to create in Rome were the most direct influence the Etruscans had on Roman visual arts, but many of their style and techniques were later duplicated. Although often at war, the early Romans looked to their neighbors in Veii for artistic inspiration. Veitine pottery and metalwork found its way into Rome beginning around 625 BCE, and a century later identical terracotta friezes were found in both cities (Grant 1980, 230). Moreover, Roman temple architecture was taken directly from the Etruscans.

As if that all wasn't enough, the very idea of Roman roads can also be traced to the Etruscans. Although some of the first documented roads are dated back to ancient Egypt, the Romans were the first people to create a true network of roads that ran throughout their empire. However, long before the Romans covered Italy with roads like the Appian Way, the Etruscan built roads that followed rivers in deep valleys (Grant 1980, 20). By all accounts Roman roads were superior since they were straight, went over a variety of different terrain, and were often made of concrete, but their inspiration no doubt came from their Etruscan forbearers.

Some historians, such as Cornell, believe that these influences were for the most part minor and superficial, but in order to take such a position, one has to ignore not only the power of symbols but also how enduring those symbols were throughout Roman history. To the Romans, the *fasces*, the toga, and the eagle standard were all vital aspects of their culture that brought the secular and divine together on one plane. In fact, some of those symbols survived the collapse of Rome and are still used by governments today to exude images of unity and power.

Roman Hegemony

Rome's last kings are normally portrayed as tyrants in the extant literature, with the seventh and final king, Lucius Tarquinus Superbus, being removed from power by a group of aristocrats. They replaced the monarchy with a Republic under two annually elected consuls. These positions were an extraordinary innovation in that they combined the roles of chief civil and military magistrates. Initially the consuls were elected by the *comitia centuriata,* which comprised the citizen assembly, though citizenship was not automatic and was wealth-based. For most of the period of the Republic, two consuls were elected each year at a special meeting called for this specific purpose. Prior to 153 BCE, a consul's year in office began on the Ides of March, the fifteenth of that month, but after that year the period of office began on January 1. The first consuls assumed most of the powers and functions of the king so, in addition to being the military commanders, they also had the authority to summon the Senate. The religious functions previously exercised by the kings were, however, reserved for the *pontifices*, or priests, and the *rex sacrorum*, the king for sacred rites, who was always a priest drawn from the patricians.

As might be expected, the collegiate, time-limited nature of Roman magistracies did not come into being overnight. Livy referred to a *praetor maximus*, or preeminent magistrate, and wrote that consuls originally held the title of *praetor*, meaning "to go before."[1] The origin of the term *consul* that replaced it is unknown. There is contradictory evidence, however, that suggests the dual magistracy was always coequal, and inscribed lists suggest the collegiate two consul system was in operation well before 451 BCE. Academics have tended to interpret Livy's description of a *praetor maximus* as incorrect and assume that although the term was no doubt used, it referred to the senior, but not more powerful, magistrate of the two.

The consuls as the holders of the highest offices of the state played a prominent part in "The Struggle of the Orders," sometimes referred to as "The Conflict of the Orders" between patricians and plebs. This was finally resolved in 287 BCE when Quintus Hortensius was appointed. However, claims that plebs were totally barred from the office of consul seem to be untrue, though they were very few in number. In the early Republic, power undoubtedly rested with the patrician class, and this caused resentment amongst those of lower social status. The terms *patrician* and *pleb* are still in common usage today but in early Republican Rome they were both very specific and highly important in the politics of the city.

The patricians were a privileged class of citizens and the term probably derives from the Latin word for fathers, *patres*. The term *patres* was, however, specifically used to denote senior Senators in the Republican period. Patrician status was exclusively gained through birth and vigorously protected. For example, in the Law of the Twelve Tables, patricians were specifically forbidden to marry plebeians.[2] Roman tradition asserted that in 451 BCE, 10 men with *consular imperium* were appointed to take on the responsibility for recording statutes in order to put an end to patrician and priestly control of the law. They compiled a total of Twelve Tables of Laws, which are currently the earliest surviving pieces of Roman literature, and these became the foundation of Roman law.

It is not known the extent of the legislation lost from that time, but there is ample evidence the laws were constantly invoked in numerous legal cases covering all aspects of Roman life. The Tables dealt mainly with relationships between individuals, but a number also covered the relationship between individuals and the state. Amounting to an initial attempt at a Code of Law, the importance of the Twelve Tables did gradually begin to decrease as the praetor's edict developed to replace them. The law banning intermarriage between the orders may have been recorded formally in the Twelve Tables, but evidence suggests the practice was already well-established long before that point. The law was eventually revoked in 445 BCE, but the precedent had been set and marriage between the orders remained unusual. The Roman class system was rigid, ensuring that social movement upward was not easy.

There has been considerable controversy about how the patrician class came into being in the

---

[1] Livy, *History of Rome*, VIII.3.
[2] *Law of the Twelve Tables* (*Leges Duodecim Tabularum* or *Duodecim Tabulae*), Table XI, 'Supplement I'.

first place and how it maintained its stranglehold on political power for so long. One popular theory, held by Roman traditionalists, was it had been initiated by Romulus. Other theories suggest Roman aristocratic families brought in outside aristocrats, such as the Trojan families who came to Rome after the city of Alba Longa was destroyed, and the Sabines, who migrated to Rome at the very start of the Republic. It was this combination, it is argued, that was able to dominate and then entrench its hold on political power.

The distinction between those of the *gentes maiores* and the *gentes minors*, the greater and lesser clans, is thought by some to have been as a result of the kings' elevation of certain clans. However, modern scholars tend to be skeptical about these explanations and argue the patrician class dates from the Republican period rather than before. There is some evidence that patricians served in the cavalry, and this would mirror the situation in Greece around the same time, when it was invariably the richest in society that became cavalrymen rather than hoplites.[3] However, there is no specific evidence to suggest patrician status was in some way linked to the ability to own war horses or to serve in the army in the capacity of a cavalryman. Another theory that patricians were the descendants of Royal cavalrymen has no evidential base. What is not in dispute is that patricians held all of the important priesthoods, and it is likely they were first identified as a group by their religious prerogatives. These prerogatives not only conferred status but often also wealth.

Senators did not, in theory, have to be members of the patrician class in the early Republic. Senators were either *patres, patricians,* or *conscripti,* conscripts. However, the *partum auctoritas,* the assent given by the fathers to decisions taken in popular assemblies, was reserved to the patricians. It is usually assumed that to hold a magistracy, a Roman citizen had to be a patrician, but as already noted, in the earliest days of the Republic there were non-patrician consuls. The monopoly of political office developed slowly during the 5th century BCE and was eventually challenged by the plebs in the 4th century BCE.

By 300 BCE, the patricians had lost much of this monopoly over the political offices of state and the major priesthoods. Nonetheless, they continued to wield political power out of all proportion to their actual numbers. To succeed in the highly competitive world of Roman politics aspirant politicians needed money or the backing of those with money. Wealth was in the hands of the patricians and so gradually the pool from which those ambitious politicians could be drawn became more and more exclusive, while at the same time it appeared that as the Republic developed it was becoming more open. The two consuls elected annually, after the very earliest years of the Republic, were always from the patrician order until 172 BCE. They still filled at least half of all positions, and some of the most important of all continued to remain exclusively patrician. These included the *flamines maiores,* priests of the senior Roman gods, the *rex sacrorum,* mentioned above, and the Salii, the college of priests serving Mars. The insistence on

---

[3] P. 576, *The Oxford Companion to Classical Civilization* by S. Hornblower, A. Spawforth & E. Eidinow (2014). Oxford: Oxford University Press.

patricians being born from the union of two patricians inevitably led over time to a decline in numbers, and of the approximately 50 patrician clans that existed in the 5th century BCE, only 14 remained by the end of the Republic. The emperors created new members of the patrician class but the whole hereditary patriciate finally disappeared in the 3rd century CE.

The *plebeians*, or plebs, was the name given to the non-patricians and comprised the mass of the Roman citizen body. The word itself might derive from the Greek, *plethos*, which means "masses." There have been some tentative theories put forward that the plebs were in some way racially distinct from the patricians, but evidence from Cicero[4] and Plutarch[5] suggest *plebeians* were clients of the various patrician groups rather than a racially separate group. Livy records that *plebeians* were excluded from religious colleges, magistracies, and the Senate. However, they were enrolled in *curiae*, voting blocks, and by *tribus*, tribes.[6] All *plebeians* could serve in the army and could hold military rank up to, and including, military tribune. The Conflict of Orders that enabled the plebs to achieve a greater degree of parity with the patricians was not a single watershed moment in Roman history but rather a long drawn out struggle that lasted from almost as soon as the Republic was founded in 510 B.C until 287 BCE It was this conflict, however, that constantly shaped the constitution throughout Roman history, and especially so in the Republican period.

In the formative years of the Republic, much of Rome's efforts centered on simply surviving. The constant demands to aid the defense of the city and the economic hardships created by the prolonged periods of conflict impacted particularly harshly on the *plebeians*. Many ended up in debt and food shortages became all too common. Tradition has it that some of the most disgruntled plebs took matters into their own hands and in 494 BCE left the city and founded their own state nearby, in effect seceding from Rome for a short period.[7] When they were re-integrated, they brought with them the innovations they had introduced that became part of the Republic's system.

They appointed their own officers, *tribuni plebs* and *aediles*. The tribunes originally numbered between two and five, but by 449 BCE their number had risen to 10. The tribunes had the responsibility of protecting both the lives and the property of the plebs. The power of the tribunes was guaranteed by an oath taken by the *plebeians* to respect their inviolability at the time of their election. The election itself was through the *comitia plebis* tribute, the plebeian assembly. The tribunes exercised their authority throughout the city and could at their own discretion call the assembly, as well as put forward resolutions, called *plebiscita*. Gradually their power increased to include the power of veto, known as the intercession, over any action undertaken by magistrates or tribunes relating to elections or laws, and they could even veto

---

[4] Cicero, *The Republic*, II.16.
[5] Plutarch, *Moralia*, 13.
[6] Livy, *History of Rome*, X.8.9.
[7] Livy, *History of Rome*, II.

senatus consulta, decrees of the Senate. Only an individual declared a dictator, up until 300 BCE, was immune from this veto.

Over time, the tribunes of the plebs became inextricably bound up with and largely indistinguishable from other Roman magistracies. In 287 BCE, *plebiscita* were recognized as being binding on all Romans, not just plebs, and tribunes were allowed to listen to Senatorial debates. Finally, in the 2nd century BCE, tribunes also became eligible to become Senators themselves. As the tribunes became more and more an arm of the establishment, their power of veto was often used by the Senate to control magistracies, but the original revolutionary aspect of their origins did not disappear entirely. Polybius claims that in the middle of the 2nd century BCE, tribunes were still "bound to do what the people resolve and chiefly to focus on their wishes".[8]

The importance of winning over the plebs manifested itself in the increasing practice of addressing crowds in the forum. The introduction of the secret ballot in the Assembly in 139 BCE meant those who sought to manipulate had to work very hard to ensure votes went their way. This was a major change in the way Roman politics was conducted and paved the way for the rise of those populist politicians who, although depending on their ability to win over the masses, were intent on their own personal aggrandizement. The rise of these populist politicians set the scene for the acceptance of an imperial system at the end of the 1st century BCE.

Tribunes remained as key figures during these developments but came to be associated with specific groups or the grievances of the urban plebs. However, as the army became more prominent in the political life of the Republic, the importance of the *tribunate* declined. Sulla excluded them from magistracies, limited their power of veto, as limited their judicial and legislative powers. The power of tribunes was restored to an extent after 75 CE, but then the positions were used by those determined to enhance their own power rather than defend the interests of the plebs. Julius Caesar, for example, was a tribune and was personally enormously popular with the plebs. The *tribunate* remained as a route to the Senate for plebs well into the imperial era, and tribunes were still being recorded as late as the 5th century CE.

The Conflict of the Orders is a defining episode in Roman history, but it is not easy to analyze because the confrontation between the two protagonists, the patricians and the plebs, took place over such an extended period, with each side having periods of victories and defeats.[9] However, the influence of the plebs did, in general, slowly increase, while that of the patricians, at least on the face of it, declined. The richer plebs became influential and more politically ambitious in the wider sense as opposed to simply agitating for plebeian rights. Once these richer plebs began to openly challenge the political dominance of the patricians, an overt direct conflict transpired. In

---

[8] Polybius, *The Histories*, VI,16.
[9] See Cicero, *The Republic*, II & Polybius, *Rome at the End of the Punic Wars: An analysis of the Roman Government*.

367 BCE, laws were passed making *plebeians* eligible to stand for the position of consul, and in 342 BCE a further law was passed requiring at least one of the consuls had to be a *plebeian*. A rule mirroring that requirement was passed in 339 BCE in relation to censors, and in 300 BCE the major priestly colleges were formally divided between the two classes. These measures were all part of the integration of the plebs into the mainstream political system that had been disrupted by the first *plebeian* secession. The decision in 287 BCE to make *plebiscites* binding on all Romans cemented that process.

In conjunction with these changes in the status of plebs came relief from the crippling debt many had and continued to labor under. Debt bondage was abolished in 326 BCE and plebs won greater access to state owned land. The most significant change, however, came with the policy to distribute lands in conquered territories to plebs. The process of colonization and settlement not only secured the territories for a burgeoning empire, but it gave plebs a stake in the Roman system. By the end of the 4th century BCE, the struggle of the plebs, at least in terms of radical political agitation, was largely at an end, and the Republic became more concerned with external issues. The lasting outcome of the Conflict of the Orders was the emergence of a new aristocratic class made up of patricians and wealthy plebs based on office holding. Descent from these office holders became more important than descent from patrician families.

The positions of *quaestors, censors, praetors*, and *curule aediles* all date from the middle of the 5th century BCE. As these offices all became accessible to both plebs and patricians, the successful Roman politician invariably had to hold a number of these posts, all time limited, to establish himself as a contender for the highest offices. This career path became known as the *cursus honoum*. In the late 4th century BCE, the Senate had become an independent body of life members who normally secured their seats by holding a series of these magistracies. As Rome's frontiers expanded, the role of the Senate expanded with it and the relationship between political developments within Rome, and its territorial expansion became increasingly important to the success of Rome's future ambitions.

After the Romans put an end to the threat from the Latins surrounding them following their victory at the Battle of Lake Regillus in 496 BCE, they turned their attention, with their new Latin allies, to warding off the threat from the Sabines, Volsci, and Aequi. By the late 5th century BCE, they succeeded in preventing incursions by these tribes into their territory and began to take the offensive against them. The last years of that century saw the Romans conquer southern Latium and begin the process of colonizing the region. In the process they took and destroyed the Etruscan city of Veii in 396 BCE.

Despite the drawback of the traumatic sacking of Rome by the Gauls, the general trend was expansionist, and the Romans' seemingly inexorable move both southward and northward continued in the first decades of the 4th century BCE. New settlements were founded at Cales in 334 BCE and Fregellae in 328 BCE, and it was the foundation of Fregellae that led to the Second

Samnite War, which lasted from 326-304 BCE. Ultimate victory in that war secured Rome's dominance in Campania.

At the same time, alliances with tribes in Apulia, Etruria and Umbria enabled Rome to advance into central Italy and defeat the Hernici and Aequi. A range of further alliances resulted in Rome being the major power on the Italian peninsula by 300 BCE.

Naturally, the growing ambition of Rome alarmed many, including erstwhile allies. In 296 BCE, Samnites, Gauls, Umbrians and Etruscans joined forces to avert the danger of Rome swallowing all of them one by one. The Battle of Sentium in 296 BCE is arguably one of the most crucial battles in European history since it was that battle that decided the fate of Italy and ensured consolidation of Roman power on the peninsula.

In the decades following their decisive victory, Rome systematically defeated and incorporated all of the peoples of Italy into their growing empire. The last to be brought to heel were the Greek cities of the south, but, as referred to above, the inability of Pyrrhus and Tarentum to stem the expansion of Rome ultimately sealed the fate of the Greek cities of Magna Graecia.

More importantly, the final conquest of Italy in 272 BCE meant the Romans had to deal with the Mediterranean world at large. The defeat of Pyrrhus was an enormous shock to the eastern Mediterranean kingdoms and signaled the arrival of a new power. The subjugation of Italy took approximately 50 years, which was a remarkable achievement given the relative strengths of the protagonists at the outset of the process. The conquests might have proved to be short-lived if military success had not been followed by the conscious policy of colonization. Whether this policy was designed initially to ensure Rome kept its hold on territories it had gained, or as a way of placating *plebeian* ambitions to have a stake in the growing power of Rome, the colonized areas soon became integral parts of the Roman system and the plebs became less inclined to embark on radical revisions of a Roman political system they were now invested in.

After the final subjugation of Italy, Rome turned its eyes eastward and became involved in the Second Macedonian War in 200 BCE, initiating a series of military adventures resulting in Macedonia and Greece becoming Roman provinces in 146 BCE. The brutality of the Roman military machine was shown at its most savage in the destruction of Corinth in that year, which also brought the destruction of Carthage at the end of the Third Punic War.

Carthage was one of the great ancient civilizations, and at its peak, the wealthy Carthaginian empire dominated the Mediterranean against the likes of Greece and Rome, with commercial enterprises and influence stretching from Spain to Turkey. In fact, at several points in history it had a very real chance of replacing the fledgling Roman empire or the failing Greek *poleis* (city-states) altogether as master of the Mediterranean. Although Carthage by far preferred to exert economic pressure and influence before resorting to direct military power (and even went so far as to rely primarily on mercenary armies paid with its vast wealth for much of its history, it nonetheless produced a number of outstanding generals, from the likes of Hanno Magnus to, of course, the great bogeyman of Roman nightmares himself: Hannibal.

However, the Carthaginians' foreign policy had one fatal flaw; they had a knack over the centuries of picking the worst enemies they could possibly enter into conflict with. The first serious clash of civilizations which Carthage was involved with was Greece, which rapidly became hostile when the Carthaginians began pushing to spread their influence towards the colonies known as *Magna Graecia* ("Great Greece"), which had been established in southern Italy and Sicily by several Greek *poleis*. These territories would become a casus belli of the First Punic War.

Certain foreign policy decisions led to continuing enmity between Carthage and the burgeoning power of Rome, and what followed was a series of wars which turned from a battle for Mediterranean hegemony into an all-out struggle for survival.

The end of the First Punic War brought a decisive shift of power in the Mediterranean. Prior to the outbreak of the war, Carthage was the reigning power, dominating the shipping lanes, ports, and trade. They controlled allies and territories with mercenary troops and gained allies and territories in the same fashion. Rome, while a strong power, was not considered the equal to Carthage, but after 23 years of war, the Romans were victorious. The terms of peace dealt serious blows to the Carthaginian economy, and the humiliation helped ensure there would be a Second Punic War several decades later.

After the serious threat Hannibal posed during the Second Punic War, the Romans didn't wait much longer to take the fight to the Carthaginians in the Third Punic War, which ended with Roman legions smashing Carthage to rubble. As legend has it, the Romans literally salted the ground upon which Carthage stood to ensure its destruction once and for all. Despite having a major influence on the Mediterranean for nearly five centuries, little evidence of Carthage's past might survives. The city itself was reduced to nothing by the Romans, who sought to erase all physical evidence of its existence, and though its ruins have been excavated, they have not provided anywhere near the wealth of archaeological items or evidence as ancient locations like Rome, Athens, Syracuse, or even Troy. Today, Carthage is a largely unremarkable suburb of the city of Tunis, and though there are some impressive ancient monuments there for tourists to explore, the large majority of these are the result of later Roman settlement.

A picture of the excavated ruins of Ancient Carthage

The Third Punic War marked the end of Carthage as any sort of city or people, and it allowed Rome to continue its rise to power within the Mediterranean. Rome's ability to soundly defeat an enemy regardless of its location was a factor for new enemies and possible challengers alike to consider.

Carthage as it had existed for over half a millennium was no more. However, it soon blossomed into existence once again, albeit in a vastly different form. For a brief period, Carthage's old rival, Utica, became the hub for Roman commerce and shipping in North Africa along the route that had once made Carthage so prosperous. But eventually, the mouth of the river of Utica silted up, blocking the harbor and forcing the Romans to rebuild Carthage so they could use its anchorage safely. New Carthage quickly became one of the greatest cities in Roman North Africa, with a population of approximately half a million.

By the end of the Punic Wars, Rome had new provinces in Spain and North Africa, as well as the Mediterranean islands. The following 50 years saw Rome acquire further territory in Asia Minor and Cyrene.

Such rapid territorial expansion could not help but have an enormous impact on the lives of all

Roman citizens no matter what their antecedents. The first effect was to consolidate the power of the new *patrician-plebeian* elite who dominated the main offices of state. The plebs as a whole were bought off by being given their share of the riches available from the military conquests. The upper classes became very wealthy indeed, and with that wealth came the adoption of an increasingly luxurious lifestyle. Hellenism became fashionable and Greek influence on literature, architecture and leisure permeated the whole Republic. The acquisition of an empire, however, was not all good news - the new luxurious lifestyles had to be maintained, and this was done through investment in Italian land, which in turn led to the creation of huge estates that could only be profitable by the use of captured slaves.

The move to slave-worked farms from farmer-soldier citizens had profound effects on the social fabric of Rome. Agriculture itself changed to meet the needs of absentee landlords who wanted quick returns to fund their sojourns in the capital or the new resorts for the rich that sprang up, particularly around the Bay of Naples. Farms became places where cash crops were grown or land turned over to grazing; anything that realized a quick profit. Publicly owned land was assimilated by the richest to the detriment of the rest. According to Appian, all of these changes combined to displace the peasants who increasingly had no alternative but to migrate to urban centers in the hope of finding work.[10] The Roman army had always relied on this peasant class to fill its ranks and displacement, but when combined with the effects of long postings in the new territories, this meant Rome's army quickly faced a manpower crisis.

The discontent of the peasantry brought with it social tension once again. The political consensus that had been maintained for so long now faced its greatest challenge. It was in this context Tiberius Gracchus was appointed as tribune and began what is usually referred to as the Roman Revolution.

Online Resources

Other books about Ancient Rome by Charles River Editors

Other books about ancient history by Charles River Editors

Other books about the Etruscans on Amazon

Bibliography

Cline, Eric H., and David O'Connor. 2003. "The Mystery of the 'Sea Peoples.'" In Mysterious Lands, edited by David O'Connor and Stephen Quirke, 107-134. London: University College London Press.

---

[10] Appian, *The Civil Wars*, I.

Cornell, T.J. 1995. The Beginnings of Rome: Italy and Rome from the Bronze Age to the Punic Wars (c. 1000-264 BC). London: Routledge.

Crawford, Michael. 2001. "Early Rome and Italy." In The Oxford History of the Roman World, edited by John Boardman, Jasper Griffin, and Oswyn Murray, 13-49. Oxford: Oxford University Press.

Diodorus Siculus. 2004. The Library of History. Translated by C.H. Oldfather. Cambridge, Massachusetts: Harvard University Press.

Dionysius of Halicarnassus. 1950. The Roman Antiquities. Translated by Earnest Cary. Cambridge, Massachusetts: Harvard University Press.

Drews, Robert. 1993. The End of the Bronze Age: Changes in Warfare and the Catastrophe ca. 1200 B.C. Princeton, New Jersey: Princeton University Press.

Grant, Michael. 1980. The Etruscans. New York: Charles Scribner's Sons.

Hencken, Hugh. 1968. Tarquinia and Etruscan Origins. London: Thames and Hudson.

Herodotus. 2003. The Histories. Translated by Aubrey de Sélincourt. London: Penguin Books.

Hoenigswald, H.M. 1941. "On Etruscan and Latin Month-Names." American Journal of Philology 62: 199-206.

Kyle, Donald G. 2007. Sport and Spectacle in the Ancient World. London: Blackwell.

Livy. 2002. The Early History of Rome. Translated by Aubrey de Sélincourt. London: Penguin Books.

Lorenzi, Rossella. 2010. "Unraveling the Etruscan Enigma." Archaeology 63: 36-43.

Macqueen, J.G. 2003. The Hittites and Their Contemporaries in Asia Minor. London: Thames and Hudson.

Marincola, John. 2004. Authority and Tradition in Ancient Historiography. Cambridge, U.K.: Cambridge University Press.

Nagy, Helen, Larissa Bonfante, and Jane K. Whitehad. 2008. "Searching for Etruscan Identity." Journal of Archaeology 112: 413-417.

Osborne, Robin. 1998. Archaic and Classical Greek Art. Oxford: Oxford University Press.

Ramage, Nancy H. and Andrew Ramage. 2001. Roman Art: Romulus to Constantine. Upper

Saddle River, New Jersey: Prentice Hall.

Scarre, Chris. 1995. The Penguin Historical Atlas of Ancient Rome. London: Penguin.

Schäfer, Heinrich. 2002. Principles of Egyptian Art. Oxford, United Kingdom: Griffith Institute.

Strabo. 2001. Geography. Translated by Horace Leonard Jones. Cambridge, Massachusetts: Harvard University Press.

Virgil. 1958. The Aeneid. Translated by W.F. Jackson Knight. London: Penguin.

Free Books by Charles River Editors

We have brand new titles available for free most days of the week. To see which of our titles are currently free, click on this link.

Discounted Books by Charles River Editors

We have titles at a discount price of just 99 cents everyday. To see which of our titles are currently 99 cents, click on this link.